To LAURA,
I hope you enjoy the >
enjoy

UP IN FLAMES

Memoirs of a Billionaire's Brat

Paul Flamer

Thanks
for your
support
Paul

Note: While this book is a work of nonfiction, some names and identifying details have been changed. Events have been recounted and dialogue has been recreated to the best of the author's ability. That said, time (and drug use) can alter memory—so please allow him some grace, and enjoy the story for what it is.

In loving memory of :
Aunt Jessica Greenfield, Robert Franklin, and
Donald Gardner Jr.

Upinflamesbook@gmail.com

ISBN: 978-1-951503-21-5

 AUTHORSUNITE

Published by Authorsunite.com

Contents

Acknowledgments

Writing is not what I do for a living. I don't like to write. I typically don't even like to read! To those who stick it out with me and read to the end: Thank you. This book is for you.

To my editor, Jess Hagemann, at Cider Spoon Stories: You're the expert. Whenever something falls outside my area of expertise, I find someone who knows how to do the thing and trust them to do it. Because of you, this book is the best version of itself.

Joy, thanks for reading an early version of the book and pointing out how, in the end, we all become our mothers. It's good, if painful at times, to have yourself reflected back to yourself.

Jeffrey, many a tear was shed revisiting our fraught history. I wish we could have a do-over. To help with your philanthropy, be able to travel, not have to prove anything to anyone, and have someone who loves me would be everything to me today. Had I been then the man I am now, we would have been great together. I'm sorry. I love you.

Mom. Oh, Mom. The past doesn't matter, because through it all, I always knew you loved me. Like me, you were the product of trauma. And in your own way, you were only trying to save me from myself. I can't be mad about that. Thank you for doing the best you could.

To the rest of my friends, family, and chosen family: There are too many of you to name, but you know who you are. Thank you for sharing this journey with me. Each of you, in

ways large and small, has shaped the man Paul Flamer is today.
I'll be grateful forever.

Introduction

I wanted to die. Nothing in the year 2000 was going right for me. Not my job (I didn't have one). Not my family (they rejected me after I came out as gay). Not my marriage (when my billionaire husband left, he cut me off financially, and I managed to lose the rest of my money in an as yet un-prosecuted Ponzi scheme). With an empty bank account and an emptier heart, I saw the ominous approach of my thirtieth birthday as a death knell. At the stroke of midnight on August 17, I would leave my twenties—and the many adventures, both spectacular and terrible, that had colored them—behind forever. I'd become, in the gay world, officially *old*, and accordingly undesirable. Why not go out with a bang then, right? One last hurrah, for old times' sake?

Setting my ageist preconceptions aside for the night, and fueled by a grim determination not to prematurely fade into irrelevance, I assembled an intimate group of about fifteen people at my place in West Hollywood. Enrique Cruz, the friend who would later help me start Platinum Motors, had flown in from Texas, and all my close friends from the Los Angeles area showed up to help me celebrate. Robert Franklin, my ex-boyfriend (and my then-current best friend), was there, as was Kurt Clements, a friend I met while living in Salt Lake City. Kurt owned a talent agency and previously hooked me up with a few modeling gigs. The only obviously absent face was Jeffrey's—my true love, and the man who'd left me high and dry two years ago.

x | Up In Flames

In honor of the occasion, someone brought a birthday cake, which was ironic since no one intended to ingest "food." A health nut by nature and an infrequent drag queen by choice, I was perennially watching my figure. Better to save those calories for the orange juice—my mixer of choice for my drug of choice, gamma-Hydroxybutyric acid (GHB).

There in the house Jeffrey had bought for me, we kicked off the evening with GHB cocktails, powders, or pills—and for most of us, a "yes, please, and thank you" combination of all three. I chased a couple ecstasy pills with liquid GHB, adjusted my Versace chainmail top, and luxuriated in being the center of attention.

In case it was my last chance.

Ever.

As the drugs worked their magic, I relaxed into the soft, warm arms of my happy place: the only room left in my head where I didn't relentlessly court the approval and affection of others. When I was high—especially when I was high on this particular mixture of chemicals—I forgot how unhappy Paul was. How lonely. Love seemed to flow to me from every corner of the universe. Everything that was broken spontaneously mended itself. Instead of worried and depressed, I felt resonant. *Infinite* as a night where anything was possible.

We blew through several hundred dollars' worth of Ecstasy, GHB, cocaine, special K, and crystal methamphetamine. Nelly's "Hot in Here" played on my Bang & Olufsen BeoSound 9000 MK3, the fastest six-CD changer in the world. Then we walked to The Factory, an ultra-exclusive gay bar and one of the hottest dance clubs in WeHo (West Hollywood) at the time. I tipped the bouncer a Benjamin so our group could jump the line. It also bought us a VIP table, including bottle service.

All night long, acquaintances and admirers (by this point, I was well-known, or perhaps infamous is the better word, in certain A-list circles) came up to wish me a happy birthday. They invariably offered me a drink or a bump—either of cocaine, or "trail mix," which is ecstasy cut with special K— and these kept me going on the dance floor while we worked up a richly ammonia-scented sweat.

Because I didn't always know where the drugs came from, or even the person offering them to me, it was impossible to predict the strength of a given dose, or with what else it might have been mixed. Typically, the only people who do pills, lines, or liquids this carelessly are those who don't care at all. Shortly after a bump of what the gift horse told me was trail mix, I blacked out. Sometime later, I regained consciousness in the club's back kitchen area, where several security guards and bar staff were trying to wake me up and calm me down. All I knew was that the room was spinning and I needed to throw up. Once I did, I felt better, and insisted that the faceless crowd of strangers surrounding me leave me alone. "I'm fine," I slurred, attempting to stand. "Let go of me. I want to dance."

Security would do no such thing. "Pull yourself together," they warned, "or you're gone."

Well, that pissed me off. Paul Flamer was used to getting what he wanted—and *always* on his birthday. "Do you know who I am?" I ranted. "I could buy this whole damn club and fire all of you!"

This dramatic threat, spouted as it had been from a skinny, out-of-his-mind thirty-year-old, barely registered. In fact, The Factory staff *did* know who I was, and they actually tried to reason with me, bless them. But when I wouldn't listen, they asked me to leave the club. And when I wouldn't go, they handcuffed me.

Three guys carried me handily out the door and down the stairs, to street level. The whole way, I screamed bloody murder, protesting the "harassment" and "abuse." Some of my friends witnessed the skirmish and ran out after me. They persuaded me to walk quietly home with them, lest the club call the cops and the evening go, as happened often in my life, up in flames.

Back at the house, I wasn't ready to call it quits. I was furious over the way I'd been "treated," and beginning to feel again, all too keenly, grief for my fading youth. With Robert and Kurt at my sides, I continued to self-medicate as only a former "billionaire's brat" can: selfishly, senselessly, and completely unapologetically. I slammed doors. Threw cake against the cabinets. Smeared what fell across the counters. Fixed another GHB cocktail. My friends looked on, horrified but helpless to intervene.

Soon, the GHB kicked in and my tantrum subsided. I felt calm and deceptively lucid. What I needed, I decided, was to get out of my head. To be sure, the drugs helped, but what the evening really called for was sex. A physical cure for an existential crisis.

Grabbing my keys, I stumbled out to my BMW X5. I poured myself into the driver's seat, then took off for the Hollywood Spa. Miraculously, I made it to the bathhouse on Ivar Street in one piece. I claimed a private room, stocked it with enough drugs to share, and welcomed one guy after another to join me. A few hours in, I lost track of how many men I'd messed around with. But it didn't matter. I was as numb to the pleasure as I was to the pain.

The last thing I did before leaving the spa was a nice big line of coke: insurance, to help me get home safely.

Four Times

It was ten a.m. when I exited the bathhouse. The sun was long up, though hidden behind the clouds, and the muggy, gray LA day felt as heavy and thick as my brain inside my skull. I'd been partying for more than eighteen hours—long enough for it to have officially become my birthday, but not long enough to have forgotten my "treatment" at the hands of The Factory staff. In the pale light of day, I could see where they'd cuffed me—dark red bruises encircled each wrist—and the sight made me mad. Feelings hurt, and my rational mind still compromised, I decided to see a doctor about my injuries. *Best to get it all documented*, I thought, *so tomorrow I can take legal action against the club.* In my altered state, this seemed like an extremely prudent and terribly important course of action.

While driving home, I called my doctor's office on my cell. "We can see you at eleven-thirty," the receptionist said. Ninety minutes to shower, change, and (hopefully) come down a bit.

It didn't happen like that, though. By the time I walked in my front door, my heart was racing. A panic attack (of the variety I'd long suffered from) seemed imminent, no doubt triggered by the past year's unimaginable stress culminating in my thirtieth birthday party. *Calm down calm down calm down* my anxious brain told my jittery body. *You have to calm down to see the doctor.* When my pep talk failed, I went back to the fridge for a GHB cocktail. I stirred what remained of the liquid GHB into a small glass of orange juice, then shot it in one go. The taste was putrid, but nothing is good when you're that hungover.

After I cleaned myself up, I woke Enrique, who was asleep in my bed, and asked him to go to the doctor with me. "Sorry, man," he said. "I don't feel well. I think I'm sick." Instead of pointing out that a doctor was probably exactly who he needed to see, I let him roll over and go back to sleep. I'd just driven myself home from the bathhouse; I could make it, now, to the clinic.

Although UCLA's medical center was only six miles away, it took twenty minutes to crawl along Santa Monica Boulevard toward the 405 freeway. I remember turning onto Santa Monica headed west, crossing Wilshire Boulevard, and then nothing past that point. I'd blacked out again, descending into that peculiar type of high-functioning amnesia reserved for GHB overdoses. Come to find out, my morning OJ-and-gamma-hydroxybutyrate downer had been a wee bit more potent than I'd thought—at least four capfuls, or four times a regular dose.

Despite having no memory of what followed, I somehow made it to Westwood Boulevard and was nearly to UCLA when I lost consciousness. Luckily, my foot slid off the accelerator and I slumped over the steering wheel, such that the BMW stayed fairly straight as it rolled to a stop. I did clip the side of a parked pick-up truck, breaking off its side mirror, before rebounding, ever so slowly, into the middle of the intersection. Drivers must have been honking their horns all around me at the idiot blocking traffic, but upon realizing that I'd passed out, someone finally called 911. I woke to the sound of the fire department smashing out my rear window, so they could unlock the doors to get to me.

Unfamiliar hands, several pairs, gripped me then, hauling my body out of the car. I stared up at a traffic light, stark against the sky, and wondered when everything had turned so yellow. When the world had gotten so bright.

"You're going to be okay, buddy," one firefighter said, but his words were far away and mostly meaningless. Nothing was okay. That's what I'd been trying to forget, trying not to feel—

until the sharp stab of an atropine shot briefly brought me back to myself. Just as quickly, everything faded to white. I was gone again, and grateful.

Another Kind of Death

Spoiler alert: I survived. The fact you're reading this book now is proof I held on long enough to write my story; long enough to put some distance between that Paul and this one, and to gain a little perspective in the process. My near-death experience didn't fix everything. Not right away. I would go on to overdose twice more—once a year later, which prompted me to move from LA, and then again in 2006, when (surprise, surprise) I went back to LA to visit friends. Each time I should have died. But it wasn't until I awoke on a gurney in an LA hospital for the second time that my ex-boyfriend Robert's words really sunk in. We couldn't be together, he told me, because I didn't know what I wanted. And because I didn't know what I wanted, I didn't value my own life. With every party, every fling, every indulgence in risky behavior, I was *daring myself to die*. I was willing to kill Paul because he didn't matter—not to his family, and not to himself.

As *Up in Flames* will reveal, I am descended from a long line of image-conscious, perfectionism-driven, God-fearing, gay-hating Christians. My parents (until they divorced, anyway) raised me to do more and be more than is humanly possible for one little eager-to-please boy, with the result that I never felt like I was "enough," especially for my mother. When I then realized I was gay (a "choice" and thereby an irredeemable sin in her eyes), I made every effort to "fix" myself by sending into exile the real Paul and replacing him with a gangly facsimile who tried very hard to will an attraction to women. This Paul would go so far as to marry a woman just to gain his family's approval. Only, this strategy was another kind of death, and a small part of me shriveled and died during those years, too, long before the drinking and the drugs.

It happened, though, because I let it. Because I bought into the notion literally beat into me with a belt that I am nothing if not my mother's son, and therefore only as "good" or "worthy of love" as she made me feel at any given time. While I now know this not to be true, there was a time when a strong mother-son bond was the thing I wanted most in the world, and I would have changed anything about myself, apart from the one thing I couldn't, to get her to love me. It's why you'll see me throw myself into the food processor over and over again in the pages that follow. I chopped up and rearranged Paul so many times that more than once, I was at risk of losing him forever. And the half-chewed mess that remained? He has—I have—crippling anxiety. Some days it's all I can do to face the world.

The thing is, I know I'm not alone in this struggle. It often felt like I was, but I've since met so many others who hurt like me, or even worse than me, who perhaps self-medicated to dull the pain, and intentionally or unintentionally ended up self-eradicating. You know who you are, or you know someone like that. Maybe you didn't or don't know where to turn for help.[1] Maybe you believe you're beyond saving—or worse—not worth saving.

But you are. And you're not alone. And it does get better. And you will survive.

I promise.

---

[1] If that's the case, flip to the back of this book now for a list of resources.

To those younger members of the LGBT community, the ones going through it now: It's innate to want your family to approve of and accept you. But if they won't, there are people who will. You don't have to change a thing about yourself to find the love you deserve. You're already perfect. Got that? Put on Gloria Gaynor's "I Will Survive" and celebrate.

To my fifty-year-old and better comrades in arms: Damn, it's been a ride, huh? I know you know exactly what I mean. We married girls and had kids and hated ourselves, but we did what we did because we thought it was right. Any evidence to the contrary we drowned in sex, drugs, and rock-and-roll. We practically *invented* the reality TV show. Then, we got divorced. Now, we travel and read to celebrate being alive. We're a little bit sad, a little bit regretful of everything that wasn't. But we're looking forward to, or already enjoying, retirement. We're feeling tougher than we ever have before. And we understand that falling in love is something we first have to do with ourselves before reaching back for those who are marching in our footsteps.

The Next Forty Years

The following seventeen chapters open with some of my earliest memories, around age nine, and trace the chaotic, sometimes unbelievable trajectory of my life over the next forty years. Winding through them are references to my favorite songs— music has always been a balm for me—and my favorite cars— the legacy of my maternal grandfather. The car, its parts, and the "rules of the road" serve as a kind of metaphor for my own journey, including and especially the times (plural) I went *up in flames*.

That's the whole point of the human experience, after all: to learn, and share what we've learned with each other. To grow, and know we can make it through anything.

1

Heirloom Parts

The day was hot, as most afternoons are in dusty McAllen, Texas, a majority-Hispanic border town a dozen miles this side of Mexico. Grampa Green, my mother's father, was teaching me how to change a car's oil. Me in my cutoff shorts, and he in a faded pearl snap shirt, we worked on his tan 1976 Chrysler New Yorker together.

"First, you have to drain the used oil," he said, indicating the steady trickle of dark amber fluid then falling from the engine and collecting in a rusty pan. "Every 3,000 miles. That's important. Don't forget it."

He spoke with the slow, patient air of a man used to working with children. The oldest of seven, Grampa Green had grown up on his family's farm, where hard work and teamwork were the only sure paths to success. Having basically raised his siblings, it had been nothing to him to later raise five kids of his own, and then a handful of grandkids besides.

"Next, you have to change the filter." We were sitting in the dirt driveway next to the covered patio that served as my grandparents' garage. An unforgiving sun beat down, and I was grateful any time Grampa needed one of his tools from the *cuartito*, the "little room" with double doors attached to the carport. There I found momentary shelter from the blinding light, if not the heat.

Quickly, I retrieved the filter, then watched him pour a little oil from a new can onto his finger. He ran the finger along the gasket of the replacement filter, moistening it.

"Why'd you do that?"

"Well," he replied, rocking back on his heels, "it helps this little rubber piece seal properly. See that?"

I nodded my nine-year-old head like I understood. In fact, I did. Grampa was a good teacher, and I had a genuine interest in cars. No matter what happened in the years to come, throughout all of the physical and emotional abuse, the sudden pivot toward self-annihilation I'd welcome like a new balm to old wounds, cars would be a constant in my life. Like Grampa, they'd show me what to do, tell me what they needed, in a language I could plainly understand. Spark plugs and pistons, belts and shocks: these worked or they didn't, and when they didn't, they could usually be fixed. If they couldn't be fixed, they could easily be replaced.

People, I would learn, can't so easily be fixed, much less replaced. You have to accept their brokenness, and love them anyway. You also have to recognize when the problem lies not with the car, but with the mechanic, and afford yourself that same grace.

For loving me when my stepfather wouldn't, I adored my grandfather. He was still a flawed man: the joint product of segregation and a stint in Burma during World War II that had left him ambivalent at best and hostile at worst toward anyone who looked or sounded differently from him. Luckily, my Mexican American grandmother was the one exception. He said it was love at first sight.

From there, we screwed the new filter in and replaced the oil drain plug. I handed him the appropriate wrench. The funnel. The fresh oil. The oil filler cap. Finally, he told me to climb in and turn it on. I scooted over the beige velour interior, feeling it catch and tug at my shorts. It smelled of Gramaw's nail polish, plus a hint of Grampa's aftershave. When I cranked the key, Donna Summer's "Hot Stuff" flooded the airwaves. After I revved the engine a couple times and the oil didn't leak, Grampa pronounced the job complete. I felt as proud as though I'd done it all myself.

Unfortunately, while teaching me about cars, Grampa passed on a few less desirable traits as well. Chief among them was his intolerance of otherness; only, I directed it at myself. To me, cars weren't just a fun hobby—they were a masculine one. The older I got, the more I would depend on them to camouflage my growing identification with, and personal discomfort with, homosexuality. I couldn't be a *fag* if I was a *man*.

At nine, though, it was enough to sit at the wheel and pretend like I was driving his boat of a car. It was okay yet to fool around with the neighbor boy and believe ourselves innocent. Gramaw Green's homemade tortillas still fixed most ailments, even the big ones, like absent parents, and nothing about my life seemed irredeemable, or set on a course over which I'd have little control.

A Blessing and a Curse

Residents of McAllen know it simply as The Valley, so-called for the Rio Grande Valley that divides (or unites, depending on how you look at it) the southern tip of Texas and northern Tamaulipas, Mexico. It was here in 1970 that I was born to Jean Green and Phillip Flamer, a couple already suffering their fair share of heartache. To hear my mom tell it, she loved my father very much—almost as much as she needed him. Desperate to get out from under her parents' roof and start a new life for herself, she "convinced" Dad they were meant to be by following him to New York, where she could be at his beck and call. For his part, Dad was none too keen. He relished his independence, though he appreciated how Mom did everything, even his laundry, for him. She mothered him as intensely as she dated him. Thus ingratiated into his everyday existence, she began to wheedle him about marriage, until the day he came home to their Bronx apartment and apathetically tossed a ring box into her lap. That romantic moment marked the beginning of their marriage, and the beginning of the inevitable end.

The reason Mom wanted so badly to get away from McAllen was the same woman I would one day worship: her mother, my Gramaw Green. As the result of her Catholic Latina heritage, Gramaw had specific ideas about good and bad, right and wrong, and she was determined to make her daughter fit that mold. That Mom had come into the world with blonde hair and blue eyes, rather than Gramaw's darker features, was a blessing and a curse. At once her mother's pride and joy, she had a lot to live up to, and carried the burden of a woman who'd never been happy in her own skin. "I was the 'star' of my mother's life," Mom told me in a letter meant to explain away her own skewed perception of parenting, "as well as her pawn. It was my job to be her representative, as if to say to all her 'Mexican' friends and those who had ever hurt her or rejected her, 'See here, this is my beautiful child. She's better than anything you will ever have.'" I'd say I can't imagine the pressure my mother must have felt to "perform" and be perfect all of the time, except that this pattern repeated itself, manifesting a generation removed in my own anxiety to please someone for whom nothing was ever good enough.

I didn't have that experience with Gramaw. She loved me unconditionally, as grandmas are wont to do. Her love, and that of her other daughter, my Aunt Jessica, would save me in my darkest hours. I'm only sorry that Mom didn't have those resources. She, like me, responded by acting out, and she, like me, was silenced with name-calling and beating. Both of us became intimate, at an early age, with rejection. Both of us have spent a lifetime re-learning how to love ourselves.

After my mother graduated from high school, she wasn't sure what she wanted to do—only that she wanted something different. She thought about joining the military like Grampa Green, but Gramaw quickly shut that dream down: "Only lesbian women join the service!" she exclaimed. Instead, Mom earned her teacher's certificate and moved to Klamath Falls, Oregon for a teaching gig. Unable to be an airman herself, she fell for one—my father—then stationed at Kingsley Field. With two jobs, a fancy car, and that coveted Anglo complexion, he could be, she knew, her knight in shining armor. She only had to make him see it, too.

Of course, hindsight is 20/20. While Dad's faults were on full display, love blinded her to them. At one point, he got arrested for fraud. He decided to take the money from the register at the bus station where he worked a second job as a cashier, and report it stolen. When Dad didn't give his accomplice in the scheme his fair share, the guy reported him. Mom not only overlooked this red flag, she bailed him out of jail. Ironically, I only heard this story when I attempted the same bad trick in my twenties. Like father, like son, I guess.

They dated off and on for a year. Then Dad was honorably discharged. In the summer of 1969, he moved home to New York, and Mom invited herself to join him. She moved in with my dad and his Polish Jewish parents, my Grandpa Morris and Grandma Gussie, got another job, and settled in to play the long game. Six months later, she got my father to propose by threatening to move back to Texas. They married at the courthouse on December 24. Neither of them knew that Mom was already four weeks pregnant with me.

This is Mom, pregnant with me.

Everything She Needed

Come May 1970, Mom expressed a desire to move back to
McAllen, where friends and family could help with the baby-
to-be. She did, and Dad followed her in time for my birth.
The doctors induced labor on August 17[1]—early enough for
my mom to recover before the start of the new school year
and her next teaching assignment. Never mind she was also
a new mom; when my dad didn't immediately step up to the
plate, she took a second job as well, so hellbent was she on
preserving a certain social status. Ever her mother's daughter,
Mom refused to be poor or a "nobody." Despite her resentment
at the way she'd been raised, she'd been programmed to "shine,"
and shine this "star" would.

A maid took care of me, Paul Douglas Flamer. I was
"Paul" after the apostle Paul and my great-grandmother
Paula. "Douglas" so that my middle initial, D, reflected my

---

[1] My baby book from this time notes that Richard Nixon was
president, and includes my health records, an empty sleeve from
a savings bond, and a certificate from my consecration at Jewish
temple.

dad's. When I wasn't with the maid, I stayed with Grampa and Gramaw Green. Grampa worked as a full-time mechanic, a skill he originally picked up in the service. Gramaw was a housewife with a lot of spare time, which she devoted to fitness and attempting to outlive us all. It bordered on the obsessive, actually, and my early exposure to her fanaticism turned me into a hypochondriac. "Oh, you bumped your head? Better get it checked out." "Don't do drugs or you'll die." Yet, at 91, Gramaw still had all her teeth—had in fact never needed dental work at all! So maybe there was something to her fear-fueled ways.

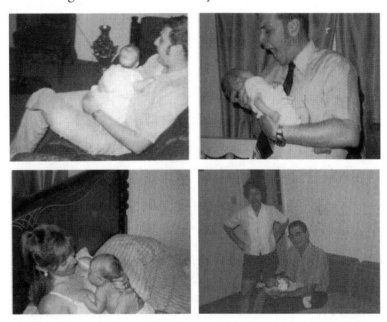

Me as an infant with my dad and one with my mom. I was my parents' first child, and my maternal grandparents' first grandchild, which maybe explains why I bonded with Gramaw and Grampa Green so strongly. My maternal grandparents' house in McAllen, Texas, was my safe space. When I started having panic attacks in high school, I would leave wherever I was at and go home, and as soon as I got home I was fine.

What limited energy my mother had leftover at the end of each day went toward polishing the pedestal she'd put me on, far above the rest of the world. Too far even for her to reach me. "I wanted you to be happy so you could love me," she said, but I was her son, not her ever-more distant husband. It's the child's job to *be* loved, not to make up for the love the parent is missing. Nevertheless, I embraced my responsibility. By the time my parents divorced in 1977, I'd been preemptively groomed to be the man of the house.

Before that, though, my brother Peter would be born in 1973, and then my sister Joy in 1976. Each new addition to our household, typically a cause for celebration, precipitated more strife, as there were more mouths to feed and mounting pressure on all of us to preserve the facade of the perfect family. I'm sure my mom and dad fought constantly during these years, but I've blocked most of my early memories of them out of self-preservation. The ones I've held onto are the odd happy memory: Dad teaching me business skills, for example, priming me to be the world's youngest salesman; or honing my appreciation of cars, as like my Grampa Green, he loved them, too.[2] I also remember the occasional family vacation.

Sometime around 1977, when I was seven, Pete was four, and Joy was maybe a year old, we drove from Texas to Florida

---

[2] Mom also fancied cars. There was a period when she owned a blue Triumph TR6, an infinitely cool car. I remember riding in it with her one day and she was smoking a cigarette. "Can I try?" I asked. "Oh, you want a cigarette?" she laughed. "Here you go." I took one puff and choked. I've hated cigarettes ever since. My other memory of riding in that car was during a Fourth of July parade in downtown McAllen. We were representing the nursery school Mom bought after divorcing my dad. Mom drove with my sister on one fender, my brother on the other fender, and me in the back of the car. It was one more way for her to steal, and keep us all in, the spotlight.

to visit my Dad's parents. I never got to know Grandpa Morris and Grandma Gussie as well as I knew my Mom's parents, though they were just as loving (and I loved them back) on the few occasions our paths did cross.[3] For whatever reason, Dad couldn't join us for the long ride there. He flew out to meet us later that week, and then we drove home together. I can still see Mom at the wheel of the Ford station wagon, leading us in group sing-alongs (Barracuda's "Heart" was a favorite this year) and coming up on the spot with games to keep us entertained.

As a child with my mother, three-years-younger brother, Pete and my six -years-younger sister, Joy.

---

[3] It was easier for Grandma Gussie to fly to Texas than it was for my parents to round all five us up for a road trip, so she actually came to visit us more often than we went to her and Grandpa. When she came, she usually stayed with Gramaw and Grampa Green, as despite their stark cultural and religious differences (Jewish vs. Catholic), my grandmothers really liked each other and got along well. Grandpa Morris rarely came with her; he was a quiet and more solitary man. Grandma Gussie flew out three or four times a year, however, and called and wrote letters in between—a practice she would continue once I left home to join the Air Force.

At Grandpa and Grandma's Ocean Drive condo, we played on South Beach most mornings, came back to the house for lunch (usually a traditionally Jewish dish: matzo ball soup was a favorite), then laid out by the pool all afternoon. Aunt Frances, Grandma Gussie's talkative and funny younger sister, often popped over for dinner. Sometimes Grandma would take us kids to one of the Jewish family-run cafeterias in Miami and show us off. "These are my grandchildren," she would beam. Afterward, she'd treat us to candy, whatever kind we wanted. Those are the little moments that make you want to visit your grandparents when you're young. The best part, though, if I'm honest, was driving back home, when Dad let us stop at Walt Disney World for a couple days. Pete and I spun in Alice's teacups until we were sick. It really did feel like the most magical place in the world.

Shortly thereafter, Mom initiated my parents' divorce. I have no recollection of how she broke the news to us, but I imagine she sat her three kids down on the brown-striped couch and tried to explain what made no sense at all. We would live with her, and Dad would be nearby when we needed him, but there'd be no more family dinners, no more family trips. Probably, I wondered if I was still in that teacup, whirling about at great speeds: Why else could I not understand her? I can't say for sure, however, because again, I've blocked most of this time period out.

With her half of the money from the house they'd sold, Mom purchased a day care center. More than just a good teacher, she had a natural aptitude for business as well. Her undergraduate degree was in business administration, and she'd go on to get a master's in education. Until then, she threw herself into running the day care business, while selling real estate on the side. The four of us—Mom, Pete, Joy, and myself—lived in the center's back room. I could walk from day care to school and to my maternal grandparents' house,[4] who continued to be an important presence in my life.

As for Dad, he seemed bereft without my mother there to make the money, manage the money, and otherwise run his life for him. He quickly blew through his half of the equity, probably on fancy dates meant to lure another caretaker into his life. Several women came and went, all of them too wise not to see right through Mr. Flamer. Soon, his pockets were empty and he petitioned the judge for half of the day care center, too, pointing out how Mom had purchased it before the divorce was finalized. It almost destroyed her when he won. Talk about literal blood, sweat, and tears—she'd sacrificed everything to keep us afloat, and then just like that, it was gone. She gave up and went back to the classroom.

Unable to support us on a teacher's salary alone, Mom looked for another husband, one who'd love her and her children the way she wanted to be loved. She didn't date a ton of men, and out of respect for us, she never brought them home (or if she did, only when we kids were with Gramaw and Grampa), but still she was always sure the next one would be her ticket to true love. I hated it. I couldn't grasp why Mom needed a new man when she had me: Paul, who strived so hard to be perfect for her. I could take care of her, and Pete, and Joy. I could be everything she needed, if she'd only let me. After all, it's what she'd expected of me for years.

Later, she'd introduce us to Dale, and that's when I'd start acting out. Wanting her attention, needing her love, I was

---

[4] I also remember walking to the corner store, called Pronto, with Pete and Joy for *paletas*. They were the Mexican version of popsicles—not just frozen colored sugar-water, but made from real fruit.

horrible to him, thinking I might scare him back to wherever he came from. At school, I became belligerent, picking fights and generally disobeying. No teacher wanted me in their class. "We are concerned about Paul's grade, attitude, and conduct," an old note from a group of my teachers reads. They wanted to know what was going on at home. Because I found it painful to be around my mother, I stopped going home after school and spent all my time with my cousins at Grampa and Gramaw Green's. If they were busy, I went to Louie's house, one of the only friends I had at the time and my first same-sex crush. We listened to "Staying Alive" by The Bee Gees and watched *Rocky and Bullwinkle* re-runs. I'd move away from McAllen and back again before anything physical happened between us.

The Driver's Seat

Dad was selling wholesale crap—clothes, toys, etc.—out of the back of a van to gas stations and anyone else who would have him when he met Ava. She picked up where my mother left off, mothering Dad as though he was her child, so naturally he asked her to marry him. We kids only saw Dad (and Ava) once a month, and sometimes every other month, then less and less as we grew older. While he wasn't Ward Cleaver from *Leave it to Beaver*, or otherwise as "active" in my life as I would have liked, Dad was nevertheless my father. I loved him for who he was[5] and what he could give, because he did the same for

---

[5] If nothing else, my dad had a great sense of humor, one I've been told I inherited. People said to him all the time how he looked like Rodney Dangerfield. "I get no respect!" Dad would shout in Dangerfield's voice. My aunt Sharon (my dad's brother Irv's wife) meeting him for the first time: He'd gotten out of his car to direct

me. Unfortunately, I did not come out to my father before he passed.

Mom helped to excise Dad from our lives by enrolling us in Catholic school. With Dad, we'd occasionally attended Jewish temple; now we were to be Christians. Right away I recognized the similarities between these faiths: Both served donuts, and both were premised on guilt. I did, and to this day do, believe in God, but He's a much more benevolent figure to me now. Back then, all I saw was another male to compete with, another person to perform for, another judge with exacting standards.

Grown-ups forget, I think, how hard it is to be a kid, shuttled around and made to participate in adults' often conflicting, sometimes incomprehensible agendas. Kids need to be protected, sure, but they need agency, too, to feel like something, even the tiniest thing, is under their control. Between the ages of zero and nine, my primary feeling was helplessness. Except for when I was at Grampa and Gramaw's, every time I got pulled in one direction, I pushed back—but it rarely mattered. I wasn't old enough, strong enough, *perfect* enough for anyone to take me seriously, or my mother to love me the way she'd promised. Instead she sought my love, and when it wasn't enough, the love of a new Mr. Right. None of them lasted because at the core of things, she didn't love herself. I saw this, and I learned from it. I, too, would spend the bulk of my twenties and thirties chasing Mr. Rights (or, in my case, Mr. Right Nows), running away from pain and loneliness, addicted to the temporary relief of one-night stands.

---

traffic at the airport. *Who* is *this guy?* she thought. That's the kind of extroverted, laughs-at-himself man my father was, and the reason I can laugh at myself today.

I wish I could go back in time and talk to that kid, that incredibly unhappy version of Paul. I'd tell him to stop, to quit fighting so hard against a world that always hit harder. I'd remind him of pleasanter afternoons belly up beneath a car, Grampa showing him how to adjust the carburetor, or swap out wires. I'd speak to him the way Grampa did, with a tenderness I found impossible to show myself. I wasn't worthy of such grace, I believed, because my own parents didn't think I was worthy—not of being my father's son; not of being loved exactly as I was.

It would behoove us all to be more conscious of power: who has it; who doesn't; who wants it; whom our now-adult agency affects. If you're still feeling powerless at this juncture in your life, consider how you might reclaim your power in healthier and more productive ways than a child's rebellion. One thing to keep in mind is that child-you still lives inside you, and child-you will forever shoulder the hang-ups, beliefs, and intentions of the people who raised you. There's no escaping that bond, just like there's no controlling other people. They will make their own choices. The good news is, you get to, too. You can choose how to react, how to respond, who and how to love, and whether or when to forgive.

My entire life, my mom was hard on me because her mom was hard on her. Gramaw was hard on Mom because her mother, the great-grandmother for whom I was named, was hard on her. They did what they thought was right, in the best way they knew how, according to what they'd been shown. I, Paul Flamer, am the sum total of these choices, a custom car pieced together from heirloom parts. But at least I'm in the driver's seat now—and you are, too.

2

My Christian Stepfather from Hell

The teenager who's learning to drive is but a hairier, ganglier version of the child learning to navigate the world. Either way, it's about spotting and reading the signs, whether on the road or in people's hearts.

Dale was bad news from the beginning. Apparently, Mom was still figuring out how to read the signs, or else she was ignoring them entirely. But I saw them: how very handsome Dale was, and how very divorced. How quickly he drove his flashy Corvette. How often Mom flew to Houston to visit him, and how infrequently her efforts were reciprocated. Eight months after meeting him at a New Year's Eve party, she moved us to Houston to be closer to Dale, sure that he'd ask her to marry him. He didn't. He proposed to one of his high school girlfriends and moved to Florida.

The day Mom found out, she took a baseball bat to the TV that Dale had bought her, cut up the beautiful dress he'd given her, and used it to tie the TV to his apartment door. In her words, she was "devastated," and I thought I could understand. I didn't want to move to Houston, leaving

Gramaw and Grampa and everything I'd ever known behind. Now it turned out to all have been in vain. I was furious. My bad behavior escalated.

I took to wandering around our new neighborhood, which was still being built, and exploring the empty houses after the construction crews had gone home. I threw rocks through new windows and tracked mud across freshly tiled floors. Most of my time I spent alone, until I met Ben. The middle son in the house down the street, he was my age (10) and lovely. Call it normal curiosity between two adolescent boys. We started to experiment sexually. At first it was just Ben and I; then a few other neighborhood boys joined us. One girl entered the picture, too, for a while, but it was clear to me even then that I preferred boys. Later, we learned that Ben was messing around with one of the janitors at our elementary school. The idea made me uncomfortable and I never joined them.[6]

Convinced that the problem was my attitude, and thinking she needed to "toughen me up," Mom sent me to Pueblo, Colorado the summer I turned ten. Her younger sister Dorothy, plus Dorothy's husband and their kids, lived an

---

[6] At Christmas 2019, when I was already writing this book, Mom had me over for dinner. "I have some old photo albums I thought you might like to look through," she said, and we sat down and pored over them together. She pointed out a photo of Ben's family and asked if I remembered them. "Yes, that's Ben and his Missy," I said, thinking *You have no idea, Mom.* She never knew about Ben, and only will if she reads this book. Mom, if you are reading *Up in Flames*: Please don't feel like anything that happened in my childhood is your fault. There's no point in falling down the rabbit hole of "What if we'd never moved to Houston?" or any other what-if, because there would have been a different family with another Ben, or any number of circumstances that would have similarly informed my character today. You can't blame yourself. I love you.

active, outdoorsy lifestyle that promised to transform me from a "whiny little boy" into a "strong young man." Skinny and small for my age, I preferred drawing and listening to Olivia Newton-John's "Magic" to playing sports, but conventional wisdom held that "real" boys played sports. Funnily enough, my summer in Colorado was one "punishment" that actually worked in my favor. Uncle Barry took us fishing, which I loved, and although Aunt Dorothy made me attend YMCA camp with her sons, once at camp I spotted a seat at the craft table, where I spent a few contented weeks making keychains and dreamcatchers!

Back in Houston, though, I continued causing problems. A year or so after we'd left McAllen, Mom shipped me back there to live with my grandparents, where, squeezed into their one-bath, three-bedroom (one of which had been converted into an office) house, I slept on the couch. "I couldn't handle you," my mother later wrote. "I wanted them to take care of you until I could get my shit together." Had she made this call right away, I would have been thrilled. As it was, I'd grown accustomed to my new environs, my new friends, Ben. It sucked being uprooted again. Plus, it marked my mother's first complete and total rejection of me, or what felt like rejection. Pete and Joy got to stay with her. Only I was being ousted.

These Blue Eyes

In retrospect, it was the right decision to make. Between Gramaw and my Aunt Jessica, I received more than enough "replacement" maternal love. Gramaw cooked me all kinds of delicious Mexican foods, saw to it that I had clean clothes, and made sure I brushed and flossed my teeth. She also kept after my education, helping me with homework and reading the newspaper to me over breakfast. Often, she picked stories to read that scared me, like the one about a man who died of a stroke after declining to see a doctor for his headaches. Any time I had a headache after that, I assumed a stroke was imminent. It's tough to live a carefree childhood when you're convinced you're about to die.

In loving memory of Aunt Jessica (center back). She has her arm around me in this photo. Also pictured are many of my cousins. When I think of the "good ol' days," I think of her.

Luckily, I managed to forget these worries while dove hunting with Grampa, fishing on the lake, and of course, working on cars. These, again, were manly pursuits, and I'd already begun picking up on the Catholic church's messaging regarding homosexuality. While I still thought about Ben sometimes, I never would have admitted as much to Grampa. He had a temper, as evidenced by the .357 Magnum he kept under the Chrysler's front seat for protection against any "idiots" he may encounter. While I did come out to him before he died, I wasn't about to tempt it as a boy. Aware that what I had done—and still desired—was "wrong," I said nothing to anyone.

A 1986 shot of Gramaw Green, Pete, Joy, and
me in front of Grampa's '76 Chrysler New Yorker.

Enter Louie, my old friend from second grade. He lived
across the street from Grampa and Gramaw, and we became
closer during this time. I transferred my feelings for Ben onto
Louie, and soon we had a tentatively physical relationship as
well. Louie was the youngest, with three older Latina sisters
who loved my blue eyes and blonde hair. They wanted to be my
girlfriends. I liked the attention and went along, though these
blue eyes were only for Louie.

Across Texas, in Houston, Mom had also found a new man.
Jim, she told me, was a "nice Christian man," the veritable
answer to her prayers. Jim's wife had left him; surely, knowing
how much it hurt, he would never leave Mom. As I had with
Dale, I found the signs conspicuous, neon orange flags waving
crazily through a construction zone. *Caution!* But he paid for
the babysitter when he took Mom out, with the money he
made at his "good" job, and best of all in my mother's eyes, he
expressed concern for her immortal soul. A devout Baptist, Jim
didn't want them to live in sin—which he promptly took care
of by proposing six weeks after they'd met.

"Okay," Mom said, "I'm ready for Paul to come back. I
want him to live with us so we can be a family!"

Over my dead body, I thought. Less than a year had passed since I'd moved back to McAllen. No way was I leaving for Houston again. No way would I accept a shiny new stepfather, some guy I'd never met and didn't want to. Here she was replacing me, the real man of the house, for the second time and in a terribly more permanent way. Hell no.

"Paul, your mother needs you," Gramaw tried persuading me. "You have to go back and take care of her. It's the right thing for a son to do." Gramaw could guilt-trip with the best of them. Begrudgingly, I relented.

Years later, and in private, she admitted it was a mistake. "I thought you'd scare Jim off," she told me, "or I never would have sent you to that monster."

Monster. Asshole. Take your pick. For one so pious, Jim epitomized evil. Adamant that he run his new household the "right" way this time (as opposed to his previous hands-off approach, culminating in his wife cheating on him), he ruled with an iron fist. The rules he immediately put in place for Pete, Joy, and me were inspired by the church but utterly arbitrary. "No white shoes," he said. "They get dirty." "Music?" he scoffed. "A tool of the devil." Michael Jackson, Madonna—these artists spoke to me. They put words to things I didn't know how to say. Madonna especially, with her 1986 hit "Papa Don't Preach" and her controversial "Like a Prayer" video featuring burning crosses and interracial relationships (still scandalous in 1989), embodied the rebellion that raged inside me. She was giving a giant middle finger to society, and the more Jim said no, the more I wanted to be just like her. I had a little clock radio, and when they weren't home I listened to music in secret. It felt so illicit, almost like I was doing drugs. The consequences, when I got caught, were equally severe. Spankings and whippings that left obvious bruises—more road signs that Mom pretended not to see.

We also had to attend Jim's church, a Baptist chapel of the fire and brimstone variety. "You're all going to hell no matter what," was the main takeaway, though some offenses were worse than others. Being gay, for example, topped the list. Every Sunday, I sat in a pew and listened as some guy wearing a dress over his suit lectured us about the grievous sin of homosexuality. Gay people were, in the preacher's words, an "abomination." It was the first time anyone had put it so bluntly, and I developed a major case of guilt over who I was and what I had done with Ben and Louie. I didn't regret my actions—they'd felt good; what could be wrong about that? So, I couldn't repent. But I could beat myself up, and vow to suppress my natural urges. I could tell myself it was Satan's doing, and repress Paul until he wasn't really Paul anymore.

Gay, and Therefore Disgusting!

Sadly, Mom's and my relationship didn't improve once we were under the same roof again. Working as much as she did, she was rarely around to witness life at home, and took her husband's word over her children's every time. Meanwhile, Jim's rules grew stricter, and the punishments for breaking those rules worsened. One day I failed to ask permission before going over to a friend's house. When I came home, he laid into me with a 2x4 board, grinning as he did so. Jim didn't just enjoy abusing me; he relished the moment he caught me in the act, the second *he* knew that *I* knew I was in trouble. He loved to make me go get the belt or the paddle myself, heightening his anticipation, sending my fear to dizzying heights. Pete and Joy were scared of him, too, but his and my relationship was extra fraught—probably because I was the oldest and most likely to fight back.

The purple welts across my butt and legs that lasted for days were outlasted only by my hatred of my stepfather. Anger boiled inside me thick and hot and red. Not an hour went by that I didn't think about running away, leaving horrible Houston once and for all. I reached out to my extended family—my grandparents, my aunts and uncles, even my dad—but they routinely dismissed my pleas for help as exaggerations. With nowhere else to turn, I learned to swallow the fear and the hate as surely as I'd swallowed my burgeoning sexual identity. Attuned to his moods, on the lookout for his whims, I spent more time in Jim's head than mine. In some ways, it was a relief. I'd entered the sexually-charged world of junior high, and the less time I had to think about boys, the better.

Two new developments around my fourteenth birthday are worth noting. First, I finally learned to drive. After years of working on family members' cars (like Grampa's, but Jim also made me change the oil and do basic maintenance on his cars), I was at last old enough to get a learner's permit and experience the freedom of the open road. Jim generously bought me a 1973 green Ford Torino coupe,[7] though he made me get a job to pay for the gas and insurance. Obtaining my license was a significant step toward independence; tapping the steering wheel in time with Prince's "Let's Go Crazy," I could almost see the light at the end of the proverbial tunnel.

Second, and not near so positive, I began experiencing intense psychosomatic symptoms: the racing heart and sweating palms of overwhelming anxiety, accompanied by digestion and

---

[7] I know, full stop, that I was lucky to get anything—but, man, what an ugly car. Even then I thought it was ugly, with its matching green vinyl interior. Part of it was that we lived in a classy neighborhood, and two of my peers from down the street also got cars around this time: a brand new Camaro, and a classic Corvette.

elimination issues. By birth a nervous kid, I became prone to panic attacks and painful, weeklong bouts of constipation—problems that, in later years, therapists would trace to life with Jim. Part of it was the constant vigilance, never being able to relax for a second. Part of it was an intrinsic denial of ego, the anti-gay brainwashing that had started in church and which I further self-imposed at school and home.

I'm sorry to say that as the result of hating myself so much, throughout high school I was pretty homophobic. I don't recall using slurs in public, but in my mind anyway I judged, and harshly, anyone I perceived to be gay. There was a guy in the choir at church who had a very feminine manner. He dressed a certain way, spoke a certain way, carried himself a certain way—a way, I decided, that was unapologetically gay. I despised him! Same for my mother's hairstylist, who had a "traditionally feminine" job. *Gay, and therefore disgusting!* I thought, taking pains to distinguish myself from these men.

From fifteen to eighteen, I convinced myself I was attracted to women (though I was never popular enough to date any of them), wore the loosest, baggiest clothes Jim would let me get away with, and worked to put gas in my car. The only extracurriculars I participated in, short of actually playing sports, were what I perceived to be "manly" ones—i.e., band and being the high school mascot. Even band was a terrible experience for me, however. I couldn't follow the music and tended to confuse my right and left hands. While I suspected I had dyslexia, I couldn't risk a diagnosis that would make me less than perfect. So I flubbed my way through, all the while making Paul appear as "straight" and masculine as possible. Was I convincing? I doubt it. But then I didn't have to be very convincing, because my family refused to entertain the alternative.

Grand Theft Auto

During my junior year of high school, I got a job at a local grocery store. I started as a bagger, was promoted to cashier, and then began working in the produce department. The job wasn't overly stressful, but as anyone who suffers from panic attacks knows, it can take very little to set one off. When your body is that tightly wound, and there's already a million circular thoughts spinning through your head, an off-putting encounter with a rude customer or a discouraging remark from your boss can make it feel like the apocalypse is nigh. Remember in 2018 when that accidental text alert went out to the residents of Hawaii stating a ballistic missile was incoming? They literally all thought they were about to die. Extreme anxiety is kind of like that.

Whenever a panic attack seized me, which wasn't often but more frequent than I would have liked, I ran to the produce department cooler. I yanked open the door and let the super-cooled air wash over me, calming my racing heart and shocking my lungs into breathing again. Something like "Danger Zone" by Kenny Loggins would be playing over the store's speakers, and the rhythm of the music would also help to re-center me. Most of the time, I could make it look like I was working, taking stock of the cooler's inventory or facing products on the shelves. It was crucial no one caught me in the throes of an attack—both because I wanted to keep them private, and because I couldn't risk getting fired. The more time I spent at work, the less time I had to spend around Jim.

All the while, I heard Gramaw's voice in my head, warning me I had better see a doctor. What if something was *actually* wrong? I couldn't confide in anyone, though, because I couldn't possibly ask for help. In my family, "weakness" was as far from godliness as you could get. The only acceptable reason for sticking out was standing out—as in being exceptional at something. Having a heart that sometimes skipped a beat wouldn't have counted. Had I been living in McAllen, Gramaw might have noticed my odd behavior, and might have taken me to the hospital immediately. As it was, Jim's and my mom's attitude was one of *Suck it up. And don't let anyone know.*

Closer to the start of senior year, I changed jobs and went to work for McDonald's. There, I met a guy I'll call Sam, who unbeknownst to me was a felon with a rap sheet. Sam and I hit it off talking cars and women. He liked muscle cars in particular, and offered to get me the hook-up. "I just bought a new car, a Nissan 200 SX," he told me excitedly. "If you help me pick it up, I'll let you drive it whenever you want."

"That sounds awesome!" I said, naive and believing I'd made a new friend.

On the prearranged night, I picked Sam up at his house. I then drove him to the port of Houston, where new cars were delivered by boat. He showed me where to go, directing us through the industrial gate entrance, cruising around to a poorly-lit dock on the dark side of the shipyard. It seemed creepy and abandoned—hardly the place for a legal business transaction. "It's fine," Sam reassured me. "Just drop me off here. I'll get the car and meet you out front, then you can follow me home. See you soon."

While waiting for Sam to reappear, my adrenaline kicked into overdrive. It occurred to me that Sam may in fact have been stealing a car; and if so, I was party to his crime. *Come on, Sam*, I whispered, willing him to emerge from the shadows. *I don't feel right about this. I want to leave.* Within a few minutes, Sam did come back—only now, he wasn't walking. He had a waxed white Nissan under his command. As its headlights played over the metal gate he'd disappeared through, I saw the mangled lock, freshly cut and dangling in the breeze.

Shit.

"Hey!" Sam said, once he'd pulled the car up next to mine. "Something's wrong. She's not driving right."

Scared and ready to leave, I told him I'd take a look—anything to hurry us up. Sam got out of the car, and thoughtlessly, I jumped in the driver's seat. "It's the parking brake," I said, lowering the shaft.

"Great! Since you're already in there, and in case anything else goes wrong, how about you drive it back, and I'll drive your car?"

All I can say is that in my panic, I wasn't thinking straight, or I never would have played along. "Sure," I agreed, and proceeded to drive a stolen car across the diameter of Houston. I watched the rearview mirror the whole way. Red, white, and blue, baby. Was America coming for me?

By the time we got back to Sam's house, my heart was pounding so hard I expected to detonate in his driveway. At least they couldn't charge the bloody pieces of me with grand theft auto. Somehow I made it home safely, where I crawled into bed without telling anyone goodnight. My conscience nagged at me for days (I've never been good at hiding the truth), then I came clean to Mom and Jim.

My mother and my stepfather were by turns shocked, outraged, and disappointed. But they helped me secure an attorney, who contacted the police, and the cops arrested Sam and recovered the car. Other than being grounded for what felt like an eternity, I escaped with my hide intact. Until, that is, Jim gave me my worst beating yet. "For your own good," he said, "so you don't turn into a criminal."

Maximum Pressure

Hot on the heels of my narrow miss with Sam, everything came to a head senior year. I began having homicidal fantasies involving Jim and the shotgun he kept beneath his bed. At first, fear of the fallout kept me from seeing it through, but after a while, I wasn't sure I felt in control. Thankfully, I had the discipline and foresight to get rid of Jim in a less law-breaking way. I called up Grampa and Gramaw Green, told them to get my bed ready, hopped on a Greyhound bus, and waved goodbye to Space City, USA forever. All the way there, I listened to Bon Jovi's "Livin' on a Prayer" on my Walkman Sport. My one regret is I couldn't take Pete and Joy with me. I worried about leaving them to the wolf, but at fifteen and twelve, they weren't helpless children any longer. They could, and would, stand up for themselves; they'd long ago seen the road signs.

As for me, I spent too many years revving my engine, spinning my wheels, and going nowhere fast. The fluid in my engine had reached maximum pressure. It was time to shift gears or risk exploding. When finally the gear caught, I peeled out with all the need for speed of a captive wild animal. *No more Jim*, I thought feverishly, *no more fear. No more pain or guilt or shame.*

Alas. I didn't realize I'd internalized these states of being. Not even the fastest supercar in the world could have outrun them. After all, a driver can't outdrive himself.

He can, however, leave toxic people and places in the dust, cut out hurtful messages like the cancers they are, and decide to be a force for good. He can remind himself and others how all of us, regardless of our perfectly deviant, gorgeously unconventional differences, are made in God's likeness. Now can I get an "Amen" to that?

While I have rarely stepped foot inside a Baptist church since Jim (and when I do, I don't buy into the message, which even today would have me burning in hell), I know and accept that church itself is not bad. I know and accept my mother staying with Jim because she was lonely, and how loneliness is its own kind of trap, making us feel scared and stuck. I know and accept that manipulating and abusing a child is never, never, *never*, under *any* circumstances, okay—but it is okay for that child to walk away, and especially when what he's walking toward is the rest of his life.

3

Valley Boy—Back to the RGV

Given my history of anxiety and hypochondria (not to mention my hypochondria-induced anxiety, and my anxiety-induced hypochondria…), you might think I'd be *really* good at self-care, perhaps even remedying feelings and situations that don't actually need fixing. But you'd be wrong. The funny thing is that while I've gotten better at self-care over the years, it was always my inclination to ignore obvious problems. Sort of an *If I can't see it, it doesn't exist* type of approach. In short, I took much better care of my cars than I did my body. I never let the dashboard's check engine light go for long before popping the hood for a once-over. The same cannot be said of aches and pains both mental and physical, or a strange inability to swallow that would crop up during my twenties. While my propensities were good for the resale value of my vehicles, they left my greatest asset—my health—in the lurch.

Soon after I moved back to McAllen senior year, I went to the beach with my cousin Brandon. He and I were a year apart in age, and always getting into scrapes together. On this day, we were drinking and swimming, already a dangerous combination, when a wave reared up over me and sucked me underwater. The force of the riptide tore my boogie board out of my hands and sent me somersaulting somewhere deep below the surface. I clawed my way blindly through the salt water, positive I'd met my demise, when just as suddenly the sea spit me back out. Coughing up brine on the shore, I tried to slow my racing heart, telling myself everything was okay. It didn't work. I couldn't get my panicked body to relax. Scared, Brandon called 911.

An indeterminate amount of time later, an ambulance arrived to take me to the hospital. En route, I calmed down enough to refuse their meds and explain to the techs what had happened. Following a quick consultation at the hospital, I was discharged into Gramaw Green's care with a mild headache and a bill for the ambulance totaling $900. Grandma Gussie, my dad's mother, had given me $1,000 as an early graduation gift. That's what I spent it on: a ridiculous medical bill.

Thin by nature, in the months after this event I lost weight I didn't have to lose. If I'd been eating small portions before, I ate even less (anxiety is a real appetite-killer). It didn't help my social status. In addition to being the "new guy" at Memorial High, I acted strangely (thanks, anxiety), and was even stranger-looking. To compensate for an obvious lack of friends, I enrolled in the high school's half-day work program. That way I only had to suffer through morning classes; then I could go to work at McDonald's.

From January to April 1988, this was an acceptable compromise. Come May, however, I realized I had no one to take to Prom, so I asked one of my cousins—Brandon's twin sister, Brenda. We resolved to have a great night together, and from what I remember, we did. We dressed up, took pictures, went to dinner, the whole nine yards. Naturally, we danced to Pretty Poison's "Catch Me (I'm Falling)," number one on the *Billboard* Hot Dance Club Play chart that year. To this day, I'm so grateful for that side of my family, who went out of their way to include me and make me feel loved. Aunt Jessica in particular just *knew* when to give me a hug or tell me she loved me. More thoughtful and affectionate than the rest of them combined, she was an angel sent to light my way. Of that much, I've no doubt.

The senior Prom I would have attended with my cousin Brenda.

My other saving grace was the 1966 Ford Mustang that Grampa helped me acquire this year. Jim had made me leave my Ford Torino coupe behind in Houston—the "punishment" for being a "disobedient son." In the end, the Mustang's loud, fast V-8 engine, coupled with a brand new candy apple red paint job (courtesy of one of Grampa's auto shop buddies), more than made up for sacrificing my first car. The interior needed some work and the floorboards were rusted through in spots, but I didn't care. It was mine and I was in love.[8]

---

[8] The Mustang had a 289 V-8 and a floor-mounted three-speed manual transmission—truly a badass car. My cousins remember riding around with me in it. I would jump the canal, making everyone scream in the backseat. That was fun.

At my high school graduation ceremony, I weighed maybe 113 pounds. I look back on pictures from this time with horror, and wonder why no one ever said anything. I was too busy working and having fun with my cousins to pay my health much attention, but didn't *anyone* else notice? If they did, they declined to intervene, too leery perhaps of upsetting my newfound sense of peace or my hard-won sense of place in The Valley. But then, one summer day, Mom called—and the "graduation gift" she gave me changed everything.

"I'm divorcing Jim," she announced over the phone. "Will you come back to live with us in Houston?"

It took me a minute to process her question. After I got over my initial shock of her leaving him, going so far as to express my congratulations, I continued to note some inner resistance. Sure, Jim would be out of the picture, but Mom had never been the world's greatest mother. The relief I felt at leaving behind the bed she'd made me lie in for so long, and the personal agency that making my own decisions had given me, were as real as they were powerful. Would I be giving those up to move back home, suffocating Paul before he could emerge, fully formed, into adulthood?

I must have hesitated a beat too long, because she apparently felt the need to sweeten the deal. "I'll even let you drive the new Plymouth Colt I just got," she offered. It was burgundy because Mom liked red cars, and a Chrysler product because Grampa had worked for Chrysler.

Well, what car guy could say no to that? Especially since my beloved Mustang now needed, in addition to cosmetic updates, an unaffordable valve job. In 1988, I sold the Mustang and moved back to Houston for the third time, where I joyfully reunited with my younger siblings and enrolled in junior college. Unsure what to major in, I took one semester of general prerequisite classes before deciding college wasn't for me. I wanted a hands-on career, I realized—something with practical applications and tangible results.

"What about restaurant management?" Mom suggested.

Intrigued, I looked into it. The program at San Jacinto Junior College emphasized watching and doing over reading and regurgitating, which greatly appealed to me. It also included an apprenticeship to a chef, so we could learn firsthand, beginning with back of house. I lasted two semesters in this program, but ultimately found it to be more work than it was worth. I didn't *love* restaurant management, not the way I loved cars.

Toward the end of my second semester, life made the call for me. As surprised as I was when Mom left Jim, it was like being smacked upside the head when she told me, Pete, and Joy that she was taking him back. I couldn't believe it; but then, her being with him had never made sense in the first place. Old enough, and more importantly, *smart* enough not to stick around for a second round, I lit out for McAllen again. I packed up the silver Toyota Celica GT coupe I'd bought the year before, and drove south toward my grandparents, who would always be more like my real parents anyway.

Rose-Colored Glasses

Are you tired of the ping-pong yet, bouncing back and forth the roughly five hours between my mother in Houston and my grandparents in McAllen? If so, you can imagine how I felt. I could barely keep up with me, either.

So, there I was: eighteen, broke, uneducated. As I did not have a college degree, and as the entirety of my employment history to date had been in the food service industry, in 1989 I took another dead-end job working for Domino's Pizza. As a delivery driver, at least I got out from behind the counter for a while. The job took me all over our location's designated delivery area, which really wasn't all that big. It was while mapping the small city's limits in my car that I started to feel, for the first time, cramped in McAllen, Texas. There was a whole other world out there. I'd seen it on TV—just like I'd seen the sports cars and the fancy clothes—the trappings of a lifestyle I thought I wanted but couldn't have.

At least, not as a delivery driver for Domino's.

"You want to travel?" Gramaw echoed. We were discussing my life over breakfast. "You want to do something meaningful? Find your purpose?"

I nodded., slowly. I couldn't tell if she was making fun of me.

"Then you ought to join the military. All the men in our family have served. It's your duty. Look at your Uncle Dusty," she pointed out, naming her youngest son.[9] "He's been all over the world. He loves what he does, and it's respectable work besides."

Hmm. I considered the idea. It certainly had its merits. My father had been a military man, as had Grampa Green. I'd learn a trade in the military, and if I wanted to go back to school afterward, I could on the government's dime. Furthermore (and crucially), the United States was not currently at war. It stood to be, I reasoned, a low-risk, high-return proposition. Still, I wasn't sold. Stubborn to a fault at times, I ultimately thought *I'm going to do it my way first. Let's see what happens— then I'll let you know.*

Because Domino's didn't cap the number of hours available to me, I worked open to close on most days. I saved my pennies and befriended the managers of the store, hoping for better opportunities. George and Jenny, the managers, were a

---

[9] Gramaw Green's second-oldest son, Jesse Jr., also served for a time, but ultimately got thrown out of the Navy for drugs. I think this is where a lot of her fears about drug use stemmed from.

husband-and-wife team. They'd recently relocated from South Carolina, and were apparently working through some marital problems. It was common for George to shout Jenny down over pizza crusts in the kitchen, and for Jenny to flirt, in retaliation, with Domino's staff. She had a great body; even *I* thought she was hot! When she flirted with me and my body responded, I felt hope. Maybe I *did* like girls. Maybe I *wasn't* gay! The fact Jenny was married was all the more attractive. It was a 'Road Closed' sign, allowing me to explore the edge of possibility without actually having to act on my feelings.

Or so I thought.

Jenny frequently confided in me, making our relationship seem extra special. One day she admitted she was sleeping with the owner of the store, Ryan. I was shocked! *But you're married*, I thought but didn't say. *And so is he!* The revelation shattered my sheltered worldview. *What do you mean, you're cheating on your husband? Do I say something to George? Would I be putting my job at stake?*

Right or wrong, I decided my allegiance lay with Jenny. I bit my tongue and kept my head down, and I guess it paid off when Ryan offered me the opportunity to open and manage a new store. "Really? Yes! Thank you so much!" I accepted, thinking only about how cool it would be to see a new town (the store was an hour away, in Brownsville), make more money, and be the one in charge for once. That I would also get a company apartment and a travel allowance were the cherries on top of this independence sundae!

Jenny drove down to Brownsville with me to scope out the store space and the apartment. Having glued a pair of rose-colored glasses to my face, I didn't recognize that Brownsville is really just a slightly hotter, slightly larger version of McAllen. Both are border towns, full of palm trees and sombreros, with larger-than-average malls that attract day-shoppers from Mexico. The key difference was that my family was in McAllen.

I couldn't have predicted how much I'd miss Gramaw and Grampa, Aunt Jessica and the cousins, or the few buddies I'd made at the McAllen Domino's store—Jenny included.

To furnish the empty apartment (my first), Gramaw gave me a twin bed and box spring, plus a few old dishes, from my grandparents' house. That's all I moved in with, other than my clothes. I didn't miss TV, music, or my favorite Madonna posters because I had no time to enjoy these anyway. Twelve hours a day, seven days a week, I ran that Domino's like it was my own small business. I learned how to manage employees, vendors, and customers alike. The only thing I never learned to manage was my stress. It peaked in Brownsville, what with the fate of a franchise riding on my shoulders.

Over the phone, I confessed as much to Jenny. "I'm just not sure I can do this."

"Oh, you can do it, Paulie," she cooed. "Now, did I tell you what Ryan got me for Christmas?"

By 1989, I was ready to move back to McAllen or quit. "If you'll take me back on at the McAllen Domino's," I told Ryan, "I'm happy to keep working for you; but I don't want to manage Brownsville anymore."

Ryan was pissed. "That's not what we agreed on," he spat. "If you leave now, I'll have to scramble to find a new manager, and you'll never work for Domino's again."

"Whatever," I said, 100% over it. I locked the store, drove the key and the day's deposit to McAllen, and told them to mail me my last check.[10]

---

[10] I would occasionally talk on the phone or have lunch with Jenny when I came home on leave from the military, but we lost touch. We've recently reconnected as she's now living in Austin and is a realtor. What a small world, huh?

Swallowing the Lump

Quitting Domino's was like nailing my own coffin shut. I'd exhausted the options at my stubborn self's disposal, and with nary so much as an opening for a shade tree mechanic at the auto body shop where Grampa worked, I set my sights firmly on the Air Force.

The recruiting office was on Twenty-Third Street. I drove there in my Celica and took the ASVAB, or Armed Services Vocational Aptitude Battery. You have to score a 36 or better (out of a possible 99) on the two-and-a-half-hour test, which I passed with flying colors. "Congratulations," the presiding airman told me. "The next step is a physical with a military doctor. Pass that, and they'll give you your start date."

Almost as soon as I scheduled the physical, Gramaw's "speeches" commenced. "You better not tell them about your *episodes*," she warned—meaning my heart-pounding panic attacks. "Just act normal and calm."

"Yes, Gramaw," I said.

Then, as if she hadn't even heard me: "Are you *trying* to sabotage yourself, Paul? You don't want to *ruin* your chances of getting in, do you?"

"No, Gramaw," I agreed.

It was like, having started the process, she wanted to be absolutely sure I followed through, and that nothing—myself, especially—stood in my way. I don't know who wanted me to join the Air Force more: me or her.

The day of my physical, I drove to the nearest MEPS, or Military Entrance Processing Station. On the way, I distracted myself with Janet Jackson's "Rhythm Nation." As I'd expected, the first question the doctor on duty asked was, "Do you have any medical conditions I need to know about?"

"No, sir," I said, already getting used to military etiquette.

He took my blood pressure, conducted hearing and vision tests, collected a urine sample, and checked my muscles and joints. Everything was going swimmingly until he measured my height and weight. "Let's see here," he said, lowering the ruler attached to the scale. "Well, son, you're 5'11" and one hundred-eleven pounds. The lowest you can weigh at that height is one-eighteen."

My heart skipped a beat in its rapid-fire stampede out of the gates. I breathed deeply to moderate my voice, then asked, "Is that a problem, sir?"

"Normally, yes. But I'm allowed to issue a waiver under certain circumstances. Let me review the results of your tests today and get back to you. You should hear one way or another by tomorrow."

He left the room so I could get dressed and finish swallowing the lump in my throat. How could this be happening?

The next day, I waited by the phone on pins and needles. It rang a few times, each time sending me into paroxysms of anxiety, but the calls were always for Gramaw, never for me. *What if I don't get a waiver?* I worried. *I'll never get out of The Valley!* Then: *What could possibly be taking so long? Did the doctor find something* else *wrong with me?*

A recruiter finally called at the end of the second day. "I have the following dates available for you to start basic training," he said. He began listing them off, but I hardly heard him. "I got it!" I mouthed to Gramaw at the kitchen table. "I GOT IT!" She started clapping and I did a little dance. You'd have thought I won the lottery, not signed my life away to Uncle Sam.

My grandparents, aunts and uncles, and cousins all congratulated me. Aunt Jessica offered at once to plan a celebratory send-off party. Everywhere I went, friends of Grampa and Gramaw who'd heard the news extended their well-wishes. Everyone said they were proud of me, that I was doing the Flamer name a great justice. Now I just had to share the news with those who'd given me my name.

In all this time, I hadn't really talked to my mother or my father. Mom was still with Jim and Dad was still with Ava. Both of them seemed perfectly content with their lives, which didn't include me much. We wrote letters, and I even saw Dad sometimes, since he still lived in McAllen near Gramaw and Grandpa Green, but now that something big was happening, it required a couple of phone calls. My dad congratulated me. "I remember when—" he began, launching into a story from his own glory days in the Air Force. He, too, said he was proud of me, which meant a lot to me, but not quite as much as it did coming from my mom.

"You're finally going to become a *man*," she gushed, the pride and the relief in her voice equally evident. "Just you wait, Paul. This will change everything for you."

"Thanks, Mom." I was relieved, too. The future may have been hazy yet, but with my mother's long-awaited approval buoying me up, I felt like I could do anything. *Now that my family supports and accepts me*, I vowed, *I won't let them down.*

Love Freely Given

Enlisting in the military was like changing the oil in my life. In a car, the oil lubricates the engine. It absorbs the heat so nothing gets too hot. In McAllen, I was overdue for an oil change. Things had reached the combustion point: either I had to get out, or risk overheating. To simply "keep on keepin' on" would have been to seize fast upon the sludge of indecision—of nowhere jobs and directionless dreams.

By joining the Air Force, I accomplished several goals. First and foremost, I asserted my independence. I moved out of Gramaw and Grampa Green's house, and away from everyone's well-meaning opinions (though they'd continue to arrive in letter form). Hell, just getting out of south Texas was a big deal. Getting to see the world would be a bigger one.

Second, I earned my family's acceptance. The cards Mom would send me while I was stationed in Europe were simple but to the point, like this Thanksgiving card dated November 17, 1991: "I love you, Paul. I'm proud of you, too!" These words seemed so easy for her to write, I wondered why I had to work so hard for them my whole life.

Finally, when I enlisted, I chose my own family—a recurring theme in my life. This time it would be a "band of brothers" (and sisters) united by a common cause, but I'd also more than once chosen a different family, every time I picked Gramaw and Grampa over Mom and Dad. I would continue fashioning families from the friends and lovers I'd later meet in Salt Lake City, Hollywood, and Austin. In many cases, these people loved me more than my blood relatives ever could, because their love was freely given, divorced from obligation.

No one gets to choose the family they're born into; and sometimes, our biological families aren't what's best for us. Whether they can't, or won't, give us what we need, it's up to us to recognize when we require something more—and to go out and claim it for ourselves.

One thing my family did that damaged me a lot, even though I understood the thinking behind it, was to silence my "crazy" early on. Because they placed such emphasis on *not* sticking out, they taught me to "suck it up" when really I needed to ask for help. Between struggling with my sexual identity and lying about my anxiety, I endured way more pain than anyone should have to. "Fitting in" is but a euphemism for being ground down, your angles and curves hacked rudely away to slide neatly into someone else's box.

From one recovering conformist to another: Please, be your one-of-a-kind self. The messy one. The magnificent one. While all of us need acceptance, none of us need to change ourselves to find it. Instead, we can pick new people—sensitive, caring, likeminded people—to surround ourselves with. And we can ask that family for help when we need it.

4

Military Man

"By the way," my baby sister Joy wrote in one of the many letters she sent to me during basic training and beyond, "when you run, breathe in your nose and out your mouth. It keeps oxygen flowing write [sic] and you don't get side cramps."

It was good advice coming from a fourteen-year-old girl, and at nineteen I needed it. Having always avoided sports like the plague, I was woefully unprepared for the endurance and athleticism basic training demanded. We started every morning at 5:00 a.m., and literally hit the ground running. When the alarm went off, we jumped from our bunks, dressed as quickly as possible, and jogged as a group to the field where the day's punishing calisthenics routine commenced. Only after what felt like a thousand push-ups, a million pull-ups, and a two-mile run around the base—all while the six-foot, two-hundred-fifteen-pound drill sergeant screamed insults meant to "motivate" us—did we get breakfast. And breakfast was even worse.

On top of being the skinniest guy at Lackland, I had one of the weakest constitutions. I wasn't used to eating such large quantities of food, though I needed the calories to replace what I was burning, and I certainly wasn't used to drinking so much water. We had to drink two full glasses with every meal to "stay hydrated," which was lost on me since I normally puked it up anyway. I couldn't go to the bathroom, either. Lots of recruits can't take a crap for the first week of basic training, because their bodies are just so stressed. Those endless six weeks ratcheted up the stomach problems I'd developed in elementary school.

More than anything, basic training is an ego check. It temporarily snuffed out the "wild child" inside me who was used to acting out and taking control. In the military, you do what you're told, no questions asked.[11] On the very first day, they lined us up, shaved our heads, and delivered a series of immunization shots with an air gun. I might have passed out had I not been more scared of the repercussions. Forget about being "the man of the house." At Lackland Air Force Base, I was just trying to survive.[12]

My twentieth birthday came and went somewhere in the middle. Dad and Ava sent me a card promising, "When we see you, we'll get you a nice gift. Not a car! Money, or something else." I don't remember if they ever did. It was a waste of a birthday all around.

---

[11] The Don't Ask, Don't Tell policy would later reflect this line of thinking.

[12] The one area in which I excelled in the military was marksmanship. I didn't have to be athletic to be good with a gun, so while I couldn't put a basketball through a hoop for the life of me, I could shoot and hit my target every time. I earned several commendations for marksmanship, which helped to solidify my new identity as an airman and bolster my sense of self-worth. While I wouldn't say I felt "accepted" in the military, the experience did allow me, for the short-term at least, to accept myself.

What kept me going was remembering Aunt Jessica's going-away party. Like the high school graduation party she'd thrown for me, this one was also over the top, with tons of food, family, and friends. Seeing them in my mind's eye, the people whose approval meant everything to me, reminded me why I was there. I was improving myself and my station, yes, but more importantly (at that point), I was making my family proud. Post-party, Aunt Jessica had taken me to the bus station, where I'd caught a six-hour Greyhound to San Antonio.

I served in the United States military from 1990-1994. After basic training, I received my job assignment—environmental support specialist—and moved to Sheppard Air Force Base in Wichita Falls for tech school training. From there, I was rotated to Ramstein Air Force Base (Germany) for my first tour.

A Beautiful Closed-Loop System

While in basic training, I'd met a brash and funny woman named Melissa. Originally from Georgia, she was part of the sister flight that lived next to our dorm. Melissa and I did all of our training together, and even received the same first job assignment. We both studied water treatment and plumbing at Sheppard, and then we got sent to Germany.

In many ways (and I did experience feeling attracted to women), Melissa would have been my perfect mate. But, to my Grampa Green's everlasting disappointment, it was never really like that between us. In April 1991, he wrote me to say, "We are glad to hear that you met a nice friend, a nice GIRL— good luck to you." He later met her, when he came to visit me in Europe, and after the only shot of alcohol I ever saw my grandfather take, he asked us point-blank why were weren't dating. Melissa found it all very comical. Although she was my best friend in the Air Force, she felt more like a sister—one I was nevertheless thankful to have abroad with me.

Mixed up with my excitement at getting to "see the world" was a fair bit of trepidation, too. I'd never been so far away from my family,[13] and I worried this post would be a repeat of Brownsville: lonely, isolating, and unkind. At first, it was.

---

[13]   As it turned out, I wasn't really alone over there. My Uncle Dusty (my mom's youngest brother) and his wife (my Aunt Sherry) were then stationed in England. There were plenty of opportunities for us to meet up when they were transferred to Hahn Air Base just forty-five minutes from me. It became even easier for me to visit them on my days off. We took long weekend trips together to the Netherlands, northern Italy, and the Austrian Alps. As Mom pointed out in a letter from May 1991, Belgium, Luxembourg, and Switzerland were all "closer than Houston is to McAllen—WOW!" I made sure to take advantage of the opportunity to travel. I also filled in for my uncle, who worked as a DJ at base parties, when he deployed to the first Gulf War.

Substitute old, gray buildings for Texas's shiny skyscrapers, snow for its palm trees, and BMWs for its Fords, and that was Germany in November 1990. Not a very beautiful or welcoming place. Once I picked up a few German phrases, though, and learned to dress in layers, much of my sense of displacement was ameliorated. I came to love those parts of the world with four seasons, and appreciate the comparatively cheap price of gas in the United States!

The day we landed, Melissa and I were assigned to Kapaun Air Station, twenty minutes from Ramstein. We each had a shared, single-sex dorm room, and we'd be working at the same two off-base water treatment plants.

The decorations on the walls of my dorm room in Germany reflected everything I held dear at the time: the Texas flag, German license plates, and a Mercedes emblem. Also present, though not pictured, were lots of images of naked women and an extensive CD collection built around Lords of Acid. I thought these things would make me straight.

Our work schedules at the plants were weird. They had to be staffed twenty-four hours a day, so there were both day-shifts and night-shifts, and everyone had to do both. Generally, we worked two days on, two days off; and then two nights on, two days off. If you were clever, you could arrange your shifts so that you had six days off in a row (with two night shifts in the middle). Working nights was easier than working days, because the bulk of the job consisted of monitoring water tank levels, and usage was usually pretty low at night. So long as you topped off the tanks in early evening, you could often get away with sleeping all night long. On the rare occasion that the levels dipped too low overnight, however, the pumps would airlock—a real bitch to fix. I had to fix the pumps frequently during my night shifts, as I really liked to sleep.[14]

That's my Gramaw Green and my Uncle Dusty.
He was stationed in Europe at the same time I was in Germany.

---

[14] Sleeping on the job wasn't the only way I rebelled in the military. Once I'd made it through the hell of basic training and mastered my fear of the unknown in Germany, the old Paul, the one who took issue with authority figures, poked his head cautiously back out through the hole he'd retreated into, and got away with as much as he could. For example, I let my shaved hair regrow far beyond regulation length, but hid it beneath my cap so no one knew—and other small, innocuous acts of insurrection. The military chain of command reminded me so much of life with Jim that I had to act out for my own peace of mind, just to feel like they didn't "own" all of me.

What the six-days-off-in-a-row scenario meant for us airmen was the possibility of having a second, civilian job on the side if we wanted. One of the many short-term jobs I tried was selling lingerie. For the life of me, I can't remember how I stumbled into this niche vocation, but it was like hosting underwear parties instead of Tupperware parties. Though it was far from the most butch straight job a guy could have, it did make me more popular with the ladies—all except my mother, who voiced her disapproval in no uncertain terms. In the same letter, she suggested I find a gig working on high-end German cars. *Good idea*, I thought, only I liked the flexibility of lingerie sales and didn't want to work for someone else. I decided to start my own car business: buying, fixing up, and reselling foreign vehicles at a profit.

Me in Germany with a rack of lingerie products
and Uncle Dusty's kids, my cousins.

An advantage of starting such a business overseas was the thirty-five-dollar-per-vehicle registration fee, far less than the comparable cost in the States. As a serviceperson, I wasn't subject to German sales tax, either, which when combined with high registration fees can make private auto sales in the US cost-prohibitive.

For my first investment, I bought my master sergeant's used Mercedes Benz. He hooked me up at the rock bottom price of $1,500—an especially good deal considering the car was still in great shape and reliable. Its only flaw was some rust around the wheel wells from the road salt of winter driving. Within a few weeks, I'd fixed this purely cosmetic problem, and cleaned the interior until it shone. I enjoyed driving it around another month, jamming to "Gonna Make You Sweat (Everybody Dance Now)" by C+C Music Factory, then sold it to a group of three female officers for $2,500, netting an easy thousand for my labors (and pissing off my master sergeant, who thought he was doing me a favor). As the women were only stationed in Germany for a few months (and they couldn't have shipped the Benz back to the States, since it wouldn't have passed DOT tests for entry), they sold it again before they left. I've no doubt they made back every penny, too.

With the $2,500, I bought a 1987 Toyota MR2: a small, zippy car, and fun to drive. I drove the MR2 until I tired of it, then sold it for something different yet again.

My first sports car in Germany: an MR2. To this day, it's one of
my favorite cars. Look at those pants, though. I mean, how
did people not know I was gay? Come on.

My best stroke of luck was meeting and befriending an American by the name of Fred.[15] He'd set up a dealership solely to sell to GIs, and he hired me to keep the lot clean and detail new cars as they came in at port. I got to drive all kinds of brand new cars without buying them, and I also got first-dibs on any trade-ins that came Fred's way. Several of these passed through my hands between 1991 and 1992.

Once a couple of local loan officers caught wind of what I was doing, they started letting me know about any repos they received. If the work the vehicles needed done was work I could do—and by this time, there wasn't much I hadn't learned to do—I'd buy, fix up, and resell those cars, too. It was a beautiful closed-loop system!

Over time, my taste in cars matured. One of my supervisors, Sergeant Wally, liked cars as much as I did, and taught me everything he knew about German and Italian cars in particular. "Only Porsches and Ferraris for me," he used to say. "The rest are junk." He sometimes let me drive one of his two Porsches, and eventually helped me purchase my first Porsche, a 944. I wouldn't see my first Ferrari until Melissa and I took a bus trip to Paris.[16] Parked next to the Eiffel Tower (and far more mesmerizing to me than the famous tourist attraction) was an exquisite red Testarossa. I used an entire roll of film documenting that memorable sighting in the wild!

---

[15] I'm not including last names to protect the guilty—and Fred was guilty! After I quit the military and came out as gay, Fred told me we should "hang out" together; as in, he was hitting on me. Oh my God, I thought. I didn't know he was gay, too! But I wasn't into him, so that was never going to happen.

[16] Ironically, the hotel had me booked as "Ms. Flamer." Sometimes, your hotelier is the first to know!

Some Things Alcohol Can't Fix

Any time I wasn't busy sleeping at the water plant or buying and selling cars, I hung out with Melissa or the guys in my dorm. While I'd struggled to make friends in high school, I found it easier in the Air Force, probably because we had *everything*, right down to our military-issued socks, in common. What social awkwardness remained was remedied by alcohol, of which there was plenty to go around. Vodka and Apfelkorn (a sweet, apple-flavored liqueur) became an off-duty hobby, and then a way of life, until we were drinking together most nights after work. It crept up on me so sneakily, and helped to calm my ongoing anxiety so readily, that I never saw partying as a "problem." Group shots straight from the bottle? Of course! Everyone else was doing it, so I did, too.

At a dorm party one night, we were passing the usual vodka around. When the bottle came to me, I tipped it up like an old pro and began to chug. I must have accidentally inhaled a drop or two, because next thing I knew, I was choking on the spicy spirit. It burned coming up and out through my nose, stealing my breath and threatening my consciousness. Whether for lack of oxygen or too much booze, I thought for sure I was going to pass out! I didn't, though. As quickly as my fear had been triggered, it merged with the catchy synth of SNAP!'s "Rhythm is a Dancer" and faded into nothingness. I went right back to partying, forgetting anything had happened at all.

The next morning, I sat down to a big breakfast in the mess hall. My hangover was ferocious, but nothing a couple pancakes couldn't counteract. I took a long, grateful pull on my orange juice—and instantly choked again! As juice sprayed over my tray and those of my buddies, everything from the night before came back in a rush: the vodka, the burning, my slender body splayed out on the floor. I felt my neck and shoulders tense up to match my throat, which was now tightly defying anything that tried to breach its banks. I couldn't even swallow without needing to cough.

What was going on?

I apologized to the guys and played it off like no big deal. They slapped my back and laughed at me good-naturedly, soon slipping into an easy conversation. While they reminisced about other on- and off-base parties, I silently took stock of everything that could possibly be wrong with me. I knew enough about anxiety by then to understand this "inability to swallow" was a new but related symptom, and one that would plague me off and on for years. Always worst at meal times, I stopped eating around others to avoid the inevitable shame. This strategy worked so well that I didn't seek professional help for it until after I left Germany.[17]

I guess there are some things alcohol can't fix.

One other "sticking point" alcohol couldn't immediately smooth over was the "intolerance of otherness" I'd long ago inherited from Grampa Green, by which I mean: There were a lot of African American men in my dorm, and right away I was confronted with my childhood programming. It took a great

---

[17] As you can imagine, not eating with my peers equated to poor "food accountability." That is, I cared more about what and how I ate when I knew other people were watching. While no one in the Air Force ever commented on my physique to my face, my family members weren't quite as restrained in their opinions. "Thank you for the pictures," Grandma Gussie and Grandpa Morris wrote in April 1991. "You look nice but very thin, try and put on a couple of pounds if you can." Grampa Green, noticing my worsening acne, wrote: "The Air Force food got you back in good health, and now you want to ruin it again with junk food!" Candy bars and chips were the only explanation his mind could conceive of for my condition.

deal of conscious effort to unlearn that bias, and at no point was it "easy" or "comfortable" work. But it was important work for me to do, as it would have lifelong ramifications—teaching me, for example, how to think for myself, regardless of church, familial, or peer pressure.

Even after I got over (for the most part) myself and my prejudices (even losing my virginity to a black female airman named LaShawn[18]), the idea of black men and white women dating each other continued to throw me for a loop. It just wasn't done in McAllen, though clearly it was accepted practice in other parts of the country, as well as in Germany. I'd met a female airman at orientation who, with her light skin, red hair, and green eyes, had attracted me at once. When Victoria started seeing Kayden, one of the black guys in my dorm and my coworker, I couldn't believe it. I tried to get her to break up with Kayden by ratting him out to her. "Look," I said, handing her an explicit photo of herself in lingerie. "Kayden was showing this picture to all the guys in the dorm!"

I thought she'd be upset, and she was—but at me, not him. "Get lost, Flamer," Victoria said, before shutting the door in my face.

Kayden thought the whole thing was hilarious.[19] He reveled in describing to me the intimate details of their sex life, until finally I met another female airman to crush on. Patty, I felt sure, could cure me once and for all of my still-very-strong fascination with men. She, too, was "into the brothers,"

---

[18] We met at a dorm party, and she invited me back to her room. All that mattered to me at the time was that I was a boy, she was a girl, and we had parts that fit together. It only happened the one time, and helped to bolster my denial that I was gay.

[19] Kayden, by the way, was later kicked out of the Air Force. Karma's a bitch.

however, and rebuffed this skinny white boy's attempts to woo her.

One day, I was complaining about my plight to Melissa, and she told me about her single friend Alexis. "She goes by Alex," Melissa said, "and she's really cool. I think you'd like her. She lives in Georgia. I can give you her address if you'd like to write her."

I decided I would. After all, I had literally nothing to lose, and getting mail was the highlight of every day in the military (seriously, even the hardest among us softened at mail call). If nothing else, I thought it might be fun to have a new pen pal.

Oh, Baby

Both sets of grandparents wrote to me weekly while I was in the military, and my brother Pete did, too. He'd recently enlisted in the Air Force as well, so we had a lot to talk about. In a letter dated September 19, 1991, he commiserated: "Bruth, you're right, it is hard." He described the "rock heads" in his flight, blacking out during PC (physical conditioning), and having to get an ingrown toenail cut out. Upon graduation from tech school, he didn't get the jet engine mechanic assignment he wanted, but became an AGE (Aerospace Ground Equipment) specialist, which I thought sounded better than water treatment anyway. He always signed his letters, "I love you and hope you stay healthy."

When Alex's letters joined the mix, they stood out for a couple of reasons. Her large, looping handwriting was decidedly feminine, yet spunky, and her favorite combination seemed to be hot pink pen on light pink paper. They also typically included a photo of herself (standing 5'9", she had dark hair, blue eyes, and a slender, attractive build), a poem she'd written, a magazine article she'd cut out for me, or some other random gift that had "made her think of me."

The letters started out innocently enough, full of the kind of "information-dumping" that characterizes two strangers getting to know each other. One letter from January 1992 recounts the then seventeen-year-old Alex's plans for after high school graduation: "I'll be going to tech school during the day, and working at night," she wrote, as she dreamed of becoming "a practical nurse" at a nearby Vidalia hospital. To me, her plans sounded ambitious but achievable—a quality I thought I might like in a future wife.

She really sealed the deal in February 1992, when she confessed to watching *Motor Trend* because she knew how much I liked it. "They say the Nissan Duad elicits the same visceral excitement and unity between man and machine that one feels when riding a motorcycle," she noted. I thought, *Oh, baby, if you only knew.*

We supplemented our letters with intermittent phone calls, and as our interest in each other increased, so did our intimacy. One night, Alex admitted her father had sexually abused her. I encouraged her to tell her mother, and the next letter I received said she had done it. "It really hurt me when I told my mama and she cried!" she wrote. "She's saying she's going to divorce him after I'm out on my own." Harboring that secret had caused Alex to stop eating; sharing it helped her to heal: "I [got] down to 107 pounds, but I'm gaining it back now," she confessed. I could relate to the stress-suppressed appetite, if not also, to some degree, the abuse.

That was May. By June, we'd grown both protective and somewhat possessive of one another, despite having never met in person. "I was just thinking about the prettiest guy I've ever seen in pictures," she wrote on June 1, 1992. "He's tall, skinny, has blue eyes (I think?), and he will be twenty-two August

17th! His name is Paul Flamer!" We started signing our letters "I love you," and talking about meeting up stateside.[20]

Highest Good

Halfway through our tour in Germany, Melissa ran over with me a truck. She didn't mean to, so I didn't hold it against her, but the whole ordeal resulted in a fractured leg and a diagnosis that, twenty years later, would make me eligible for disability.

Basically, Melissa was driving a buffalo truck (a giant water delivery vehicle) the day we were carrying water to another off-site station, fifteen miles or so away from our plant. I hopped out to open the gates, so she could back the truck into the site, only I hadn't quite finished when she started backing up. She couldn't hear me yell over the monstrous diesel engine, and managed to pin me between the truck's bumper and the half of the gate still bolted to the ground. Luckily, the mesh of the gate gave way, bending with my body and saving my vital organs, but where my left leg hooked over the gate's steel frame, it was crushed. Sensing the resistance, but not realizing what was happening, Melissa accelerated, eventually wrenching the gatepost free of the ground and flinging it, and me, several feet

---

[20] Meanwhile, back in Texas, Mom had left Jim for the second and last time (thank God), and she, too, seemed to have met someone new. Like Jim, this guy was also a pious church-goer, though of a more progressive persuasion. "I feel like I'm in heaven," her Easter card said. "We have a great time together—we've gone dancing twice already! Am I happy? Oh yes. And it's about time!" I wanted to be happy for her, but I couldn't, not really. I was more concerned with my own blossoming relationship, and besides, I no longer trusted her judgment.

behind the truck. Well, that got her attention. She immediately called for help and an ambulance soon arrived. At first, I couldn't feel anything, but when they took my boot off on the way to the hospital, I screamed. I passed in and out of consciousness until they reset my leg and immobilized it in a full-length cast. On the doctor's recommendation, I received three weeks' convalescent leave.

Figuring I'd recuperate faster among family, I left base for Uncle Dusty's and Aunt Sherry's house. Someone saw me driving and reported me to the commander. "If Flamer can drive a car," the anonymous tattle-tale said, "he can work light duty at the water plant." Three days after I'd settled onto my aunt's couch, the base called and told me to come back. I fought it—I had papers from the doctor, after all—but the military really does own you. I not only had to return to work, but my "insubordination" cost me a promotion to senior airman.

Here's my commander pinning my second stripe. Following the incident with the buffalo truck, I never got a third stripe.

Fast-forward to the end of our tour. I was walking again, and Melissa's and my friendship was likewise back on solid footing, when she started dating a real asshole of a guy from our dorm. He liked to control who she was and wasn't allowed to see; I was on the "not allowed" list, obviously. I tried to talk some sense into her, but love blinds the best of us sometimes. She ended up marrying the jerk, though she divorced him after he threw a telephone at her head.

One of the last conversations Melissa and I had at Ramstein involved our decision to swap assignments in the States. I'll remind you here that Melissa was from Georgia. My orders were to report to Robins Air Force Base in Georgia, while Melissa was being sent to Hill Air Force Base in Utah. "Would you trade with me?" she wanted to know. "Robins is really close to where my family lives, and I'd like to go back home."

Since neither Georgia nor Utah was close to home for me, I had no preference and applied for the swap. It was approved, and my fate was determined: I'd spend the next two years in northern Utah, at a picturesque base sandwiched between Ogden to the north and Salt Lake City to the south.

I couldn't have known then how that single decision, seemingly so insignificant, would change the course of my life. Already, I'd narrowly missed deploying to the first Gulf War (a resolution, passed two days before we shipped out, resulted in me receiving a medal without ever going to war); what further difference could choosing a western state over a southern one make? But it did. It made all the difference! Life as I know it now started for me in Utah. It began with a woman. And ended with a man.

Today I believe that "accidents" don't exist—that everything in life happens for a reason, and exactly as it's supposed to. We get in the way sometimes, mucking up the universe's plans for us because we can't see them clearly yet, but fate always prevails. Fortunately, I also believe fate and/or the universe is always working toward our highest good. Life's not a random chain of events, but a series of baby steps so small they might not even register as progress—until you look back, later, and see how it all makes sense. For without pain, we can't know pleasure; and periods of stagnation, loneliness, or turmoil in truth prepare us for our greatest happiness.

5

Back to the USA

With two weeks between the afternoon I left Germany and the morning I had to report to Hill Air Force Base in Utah, I decided to visit my paternal grandparents in Florida, meet Alex in Georgia, then wind my way west toward everyone else in Texas. It would be a welcome "reunion tour" after two long years abroad, and, I hoped, the emotional nourishment I would need to tackle another new post, in another new place, with its own set of challenges and opportunities.

When I touched down at Miami International Airport, I caught a cab straight to the local Mazda dealership. At Ramstein, I'd had Grandma Gussie send me the Sunday classifieds, so I knew what vehicles were available in their area, and I had my eye on a gold '91 Mazda MX-3 (gold, it should be noted, is my least favorite color; however, the MX-3's V6 engine, five-speed transmission, and sunroof, not to mention the remarkably low mileage for being a pre-owned, outweighed the unfortunate paint job). I took the nearly $15,000 I'd managed to save from my side hustles abroad and bought my first sports car of that model. Believe me when I say that, in 1992, it was one sweet car!

My paternal grandparents' Ocean Drive condo overlooking
Miami Beach. That's my dear Grandma Gussie.

Grandma Gussie didn't quite see it that way. Having fled
Poland to escape the pogroms (mass killings of Jews by attack
mobs terrorizing eastern Europe from the late 1800s through
the early 1930s, right up until the Nazis came to power), she was
intimately familiar with the crippling poverty that besets most
immigrants upon their arrival to this country. In her old age,
her pantry overflowed with restaurant packets of ketchup, salt,
and sugar, and her kitchen drawers were stuffed full of straws
and toothpicks—the kind of "nonessential" condiments and
accoutrements that only someone who's survived tremendous
hardship now religiously keeps on hand at all times. She was
never happier than when one of her grandchildren needed
mustard, and she had some at the ready. We kids had our
secret laughs about it, but to this day, I still take an extra straw
or packet of sauce from the restaurant, just in case. I do not,
however, share her conscientious frugality—which my purchase
of an expensive sports car directly flouted.

Although she never admitted as much, opting instead for
the politically neutral "Enjoy it in good health," Grandma
did not approve of my spending more than my annual take-
home pay in one sitting, and on something arguably more
"nonessential" than utilitarian straws. To be fair, she'd never

owned a car—or even driven one, that I know of—so I couldn't expect her to understand the sheer joy the MX-3 brought me. I couldn't wait to drive it cross-country: a prime opportunity to revisit Queen's "Bohemian Rhapsody" and sing along at the top my lungs. First, though, I spent several days with my dear paternal grandparents.

Grandma made the most of our short time together by taking me to visit all of her friends, and showing me off to everyone we met. The way she gushed about my personality and accomplishments made me feel proud and loved; I was always "good enough" for Grandma Gussie. With Grandpa, I sat on South Beach and listened to the waves, and felt some of my uneasiness about my next post slip away. I slept soundly each night on the sofa in their living room—and then it was on to Georgia.

Sexy Time

Something weird started to happen near the end of my time in Germany that made meeting Alex in person an even bigger deal. Men, both military and civilian, had begun catcalling me as I walked past, and leaving notes on my car with suggestive messages. The notes ranged from the friendly "Hey, wanna hang out?" to the no-holds-barred "Meet me in the bathroom at 10 PM." To my knowledge, I wasn't doing or saying anything to attract this kind of attention, so I convinced myself it was a test. While the now-infamous Don't Ask, Don't Tell policy wouldn't pass for another eighteen months, you could still be kicked out unofficially for being gay, and that's what I thought these guys were doing—trying to get me in trouble, though for what reason I didn't know.

It's possible some of them really were interested in me; that on some level, they could tell I was "different" and they wanted a taste. And to be sure, I found some of them cute as well! Afraid of jeopardizing my career, however, and still certain that with enough time and practice I could make myself want women, I ignored the whistles and threw the notes away. I gave myself what in car lingo we call a "tune-up"—a bit of "preventative maintenance" to keep myself and my life running smoothly—by which I mean: I only dated women in Germany, and then stayed loyal to Alex once we decided to be exclusive. Changing my sexual predilections through sheer force of will, I reasoned, was no different from changing the coolant of my Mercedes. It would, in other words, keep everything from blowing up.

Almost without meaning to, I put a lot of pressure on myself to get Alex's and my relationship "right," to the extent I was already thinking about proposing if things went well during our first visit. We got along so sublimely long-distance; surely we'd have face-to-face chemistry, too. On the appointed weekend, Melissa was kind enough to let us use her dorm room on Robins Air Force Base. Alex's parents didn't approve of our relationship (we had reason to believe they were intercepting my letters to her, "or maybe there's just a hole in our mailbox," Alex half-joked in an undated letter from around this time), so we skirted them entirely by meeting somewhat clandestinely. I remember walking into that dorm room, seeing a tall, lithe, and very attractive woman stand up to shake my hand, and feeling the same way my mother had felt about me joining the Air Force: excited and relieved in equal measure. This was going to work.

Melissa made herself scarce so Alex and I could have sexy time. The sex was, and would continue to be, surprisingly good. Before we parted, I talked to her about getting married. "Once I get settled in Utah," I said, "you could come live with me on base. We'd qualify for married housing, which is nicer than Melissa's room." I waved broadly at her drab walls and shared bathroom. "And once we're legal, your parents won't be able to say a thing. Just think about it, okay?"

Alex didn't need to think about it. She accepted right away. Was it all a little strange, and a little soon? Absolutely. Should I have listened to the voice in my head warning me how I barely knew this woman—how I was in love not with her, but with a fantasy? Yes! But to do so would have meant acknowledging the other, related voice insisting I was gay, and I'd stuffed that voice down as far as it would go. Alex was hot. She seemed nice. My family would like her. They'd applaud my smart choice, commend me for "living right in the eyes of God," and never know about my sexuality. Alex would be out of her parents' house and away from her abusive father. Everyone would win!

From this point on, we corresponded strictly through Melissa so Alex's parents couldn't discover and intervene in our plans. I sent my letters for Alex to Melissa, who either passed them on directly or included them in her own letters to Alex, and Alex mailed my letters to Melissa, who then forwarded them on to me. The chance Alex was taking to remain in communication with me while still under her controlling father's roof meant a lot to me. It made me feel loved and wanted in a way I'd always hoped for but never experienced.

With our decision made, and fairly bursting with the biggest news I'd ever had to share, I drove the Mazda MX-3 on to Texas.

Strawberries and Cream

It took two days to drive the more than 1,200 miles between Vidalia and McAllen. I entertained myself by pushing the MX-3's manual transmission to its limits, alternately slowing the vehicle down to a crawl and accelerating as quickly as possible. Each time, I kept the gas pedal pinned to the floor until the tachometer nearly hit the red line on the gauge, then shifted at the last moment into the next highest gear. The upgraded V6 motor, far superior to the anemic, four-cylinder base model, delivered in a big way. Between the thrilling speed (it's a miracle I didn't get a ticket, or get arrested for reckless driving) and the heady challenge of engaging the clutch just before it cut out the motor, the miles flew by.

Back home, I couldn't wait to see everyone, show off my new car, and bathe in their adulation, secure in the knowledge that, finally, Paul had it all together. Not only was I, by all appearances, "thriving" in the military, but I was engaged to a beautiful, Christian, God-fearing woman who checked all of my mother's boxes. What more could anyone want? Sitting around the dinner table that evening, however, surrounded by everyone who loved me—Grampa and Gramaw Green, my mother, my brother, my sister, and all of my cousins—something held me back. I readily shared stories from Germany (they hung on every word), and answered as many of their questions as I could about Utah (a place I'd not yet seen), but three platefuls of chicken fajitas (topped with Gramaw's signature guacamole and pico de gallo!) and two glasses of sweet tea later, I still hadn't breathed a word about Alex. I think I was afraid of admitting I'd only met her once, aware of how it would sound and sure there'd be an uproar.[21]

As it was, my family's happiness for me shone on their faces, and I didn't dare do anything to disrupt it. *Anyway, there's time,* I consoled myself. *I'm here for a week. The right way to bring up my impending marriage will present itself.* So I asked them about

---

[21] What if they talked me out of it, thereby (paradoxically) ruining my one shot at becoming the man they wanted me to be? No; I needed to *show* them what was good for me, and by extension, them. Asking their permission—or even giving them a heads-up—would have denied me the opportunity to prove I was right.

their lives instead, and listened to Gramaw harangue me in her typically loving-but-critical way. "Are you working out, Paul? You should hang around the gym and build your body," she said. Or her favorite threatening reminder, bandied about any time I mentioned goofing off on-base: "You don't want to get thrown out of the Air Force, do you?" Her well-intentioned nagging made me nostalgic for the years I'd lived with her and Grampa. At the same time, it made me realize I was no longer the nine-year-old who'd rolled beneath Grampa's '76 Chrysler on a mechanic's creeper. I was growing up, and making grown-up decisions, the consequences of which would be mine alone to bear.

At the end of my week home, Aunt Jessica threw her usual celebratory send-off party.[22] Her living room was decorated for Christmas, with festive green and red tinsel on the tree, and a nativity set atop the piano. "Rockin' around the Christmas Tree," my favorite Christmas song, played on repeat. The tantalizing smells of brisket and homemade tortillas greeted everyone who walked through the door, and no one went home without an extra slice of white cake topped with strawberries and cream. There were enough pickings left on the meat-and-cheese trays to feed a small army, which Aunt Jessica and I grazed on long into the night. We visited, laughed, and enjoyed life and each other, and still I failed to mention Alex. I did what I had become all too good at—keeping a secret.

---

[22] As kids, we thought these parties were Aunt Jessica's way of "sharing the wealth." Her husband, Uncle Benny, worked full time as a border patrol agent (eventually becoming a US Marshall), and we knew his mother owned some oil wells. I later found out Aunt Jessica lived payday to payday just like our family. She was frugal with her money, and made sacrifices in her own life, simply because she loved throwing parties for her extended family so much. This revelation made me appreciate her warmth and generosity even more.

I was sad to leave, but also anxious to hit the road again, both for a chance to drive the MX-3 some more and to say hello to my new home for the next two years. I left on December 28, and set eyes on Hill Air Force Base (and the beautiful mountains of Layton, Utah) December 30, 1992.

Man, Behold Your Wife!

Hill Air Force Base, literally named for its geographic position on a hill, combined the snowy, bracing winters of Germany with the comforting McStaples of everyday American life. Driving in along Interstate 15, mountains reared up to my left and right, and stretched as far as the eye could see. I would get to enjoy all four seasons here, as well as life in the neighboring pristine capital, Salt Lake City. Although Utah had never been on my list of places to visit (*other than praying and skiing, what the hell goes on in Utah?* I wondered), between the awe-inspiring landscape and the people I would meet there, it became one of my favorite states. Salt Lake City itself, its conservative, Mormon-centric culture notwithstanding, was vibrant and alive, and it made me feel that way, too.

When I checked into Hill, I was assigned a private dorm room with a shared bathroom. It meant that while the other bunk in my room remained empty, I nevertheless shared a shower and a toilet with the two airmen in the double room next-door. I looked forward to meeting them. *Would they be hot?* I mused. As it turned out, they weren't—and then I chided myself for even thinking such thoughts. *You're engaged to marry Alex!* I scolded twenty-two-year-old Paul. *Snap out of it!*

The dorms at Layton weren't nearly as nice as those in Germany had been, though they were closer to work than my commute from Kapaun. A short five-minute drive to the industrial water treatment plant equaled more time to sleep in, which I needed since my job in Utah was harder. Gone were the days of idly adding chlorine and fluoride to clean city water; at Layton, I'd be handling hazardous wastewater direct from the flight line, where mechanical repairs were performed on fighter jets. My duties essentially included shoveling the resultant toxic sludge, polluted with cyanide and other heavy metals, into a honeycomb-shaped sludge press, which squeezed the water from the sludge so it could be reclaimed and cleaned at the city water plant. The leftover sludge then dried into dirt, which we packed into industrial containers for haul-away by eighteen-wheelers. Throughout this back-breaking process, we were supposed to wear respirators, bulky aprons, gloves, and ear plugs against the dangerous off-gassing and overwhelming noise, but I didn't always, and now have tinnitus as a result. It could be worse, though.

In my limited downtime, I wrote to Alex (we were hashing out a plan to get her to Utah), explored my new hometown, and made some new friends. One of the first and closest friends I would make was named Leif—a man as handsome and Nordic as his name might imply. Tall, muscular, and about my age, Leif was also relatively new to the plant, having arrived on base shortly before me. We bonded over cars, and while I eagerly listened to him vent about his unsupportive wife, Syd, and cooed over photos of their one-year-old daughter, really I was just soaking him up, basking in the sunshine of my first crush since Louie. And what a debilitating crush it was! I found myself wanting to spend every spare moment with him, whether on the job or going out for drinks afterward. I even saw a psychiatrist to work on my swallowing issues, just so Leif and I could eat in the mess hall together. My doctor put me on Klonopin, a drug used to treat panic attacks that works by calming your brain and nerves. It was the first prescription medicine I would take, though far from the last, for a variety of symptoms over the next twenty years.

Through the end of January 1993, I worked hard, saved my money, and nursed a secret love for Leif. Only once things became unbearable at home for Alex—and it seemed like Leif's marriage might work out after all—did I send for my fiancé, finally ready to tie the knot and commit to living (what even then I refused to acknowledge as) a lie. I mailed Alex the money for a bus ticket. Our mutual friend Melissa helped get her to the station. At the last minute, Alex's father discovered her late-night escape plan and chased her out of the house with a knife, but Melissa was waiting and saw her safely downtown. From there, Alex caught a series of Greyhounds that slowly trundled west. She called me from each new station to give me a status update, and the closer she got, the greater my anxiety grew. I just wasn't sure marrying her was the right thing to do. On one hand, almost everyone I knew was married. Marriage was "part of God's plan," a good and holy institution that joined two lovers and united whole families. But why, then, had I still not told my family?

"Okay," I said to Alex, after every time she checked in. "Thanks for letting me know. Can't wait to see you. I love you." I would hang up the phone and pop another Klonopin—anxious to quell the sick feeling, via the most readily available means, that I was making the worst mistake of my life.

At the appointed time, two-and-a-half days after Alex left Georgia, I went to meet her at the bus station. I brought her a bouquet of flowers and showed up in my best military dress, resolved not to let my external appearance betray the scared kid inside. She jumped off the bus and into my arms with nothing but a backpack full of dreams. If she was my chance to "marry the gay away," I was her literal ticket out—out of Vidalia and into the unknown, where anything would be possible for both of us. It was, as Melissa later called it, a reciprocal "marriage of convenience," though early on, anyway, we deluded ourselves into believing it was something more.

As soon as I saw her smile, her clear blue eyes and her rosy cheeks even prettier than I remembered, I relaxed. As it had when we'd spent a weekend together in Georgia, my body responded to her trim, boyish figure. I felt excited, not anxious; lucky, not doomed. I escorted my would-be wife to the car, and we drove straight to the justice of the peace. Outside the courthouse, our awkward silence gave way to giddiness. Man, behold your wife! Woman, behold your husband!

After saying our vows, I took Alex to our new home— temporary housing I had arranged in advance with my marriage allotment. It was spartan as a motel room, but we couldn't see that through our glee. This night marked the beginning of the rest of our lives; as such, it called for a celebration. We laughed, drank champagne, and made love like sloppy teenagers, consumed by the other's body, touch, taste. February nights get cold in Utah, but we had zero problem keeping warm. *What*, I marveled, *had I been so worried about?* Married life was off to a great start!

And I hadn't even thought about Leif once.

Sludge City

Best of all, something about the words "I do" freed me to break the news to my family. It was as though, newly shackled with my own "ball and chain," I was now *less* of a prisoner to fear and doubt. I no longer had to seek my family's acceptance or society's approval; someone in Utah loved me! She'd legally joined her life to mine! What could anyone say or do to undermine that fact? Nothing!

So, I called up Mom. "Guess what?" I shouted, jubilant. "I got married! Her name is Alex!" It took my mother some time to process this information. Her shock evolved into fifty thousand questions, became a kind of dumbfounded happiness. *Paul has found someone with whom to spend the rest of his life. My baby boy is married!* Mom and Gramaw both said they couldn't wait to meet her. "You'll spend next Christmas in Texas," they echoed—a command, not an invitation.

Everything had fallen into place. I had a career, a wife, and my family's love, all of which genuinely fulfilled me. My friends were supportive, if distracting (Leif), my car was still the coolest I'd ever owned, and my anxiety at last appeared under control. In just a few short years, I'd gone from delivering Domino's pizzas to serving my country; from idling at the terminus of a dead-end road to cruising down the interstate with a beautiful woman at my side.

It would take even less time for everything to fall apart.

Like a fuel additive that promises performance, only to turn your gas tank into Sludge City, reader, beware those people, places, and things that seem too good to be true. Should you find yourself pinching your arm at your good fortune, chances are you're not living the dream, but stuck in a dream—one that's liable to become a nightmare. I'm not saying "Don't risk it" or telling you to hold back. On the contrary: I want you to be present for the happiest moments of your life. If they turn out not to be so happy, though, I'll bet that on reconsideration, you can spot the second when you squelched your inner voice, told intuition to take a hike, and hit the accelerator; the instant, in other words, when you turned traitor on yourself. How close did you nudge the tachometer to the red zone? Did you slow down before it was too late, or drive like a madman until your engine gave up the ghost?

I stayed in my marriage for longer than I should have, especially given how every ounce of me had railed against marrying Alex before it even happened. Importantly, I don't blame her. We were young and misguided, and it was never going to work. I was always going to redline forcing myself to be someone I was not. No engine—no body—can sustain that pressure indefinitely. Inevitably, I would come to a complete halt, and watch, a helpless bystander, as my life went up in *actual* flames, before I could overhaul my engine and get back on track.

6

Mazda Mishap

I liked my wife. Really, I did. For a month, we had crazy sex, multiple times a day, and pillow-talked in between about the life we were building together. In her letters to me, Alex had expressed a deep desire to be a wife and homemaker, in addition to her nursing school goals, and she did not disappoint. She made our temporary residence as warm and inviting as possible, and when we moved to married housing in Ogden, a railroad town ten miles from base, she transformed that space, too. Leif and his wife Syd helped us locate a home for rent just a few doors down from theirs. Amazingly, Alex and Syd hit it off right away. The four of us, all with traditionally male names and ulterior motives, "double-dated" frequently. Everyone enjoyed these outings, but none so much as me, seated between my loving wife on one side and my rampant crush on the other.

Soon, Leif's and Syd's marriage hit a rough patch again. As he had before, and as my old boss Jenny had before him, Leif confided in me, making me feel trusted and special. While I hated to see him so sad, I loved being the one to comfort him. Each time he and Syd fought only intensified his and my friendship, and my ongoing infatuation with Leif. I also learned from him what to watch out for in marriage; for example, how Syd used their child like a bargaining chip. "She threatens to leave me on a weekly basis," Leif admitted. "She says she's going back to California, and taking our daughter with her." His situation made me rethink my own. *Best not to introduce children too early*, I concluded, though Alex had already begun pressuring me on this very topic. Since our wedding night, I'd instinctively and consistently used condoms, never giving the "why" much thought. Now I asked her to start taking birth control pills as well—an extra safeguard she neither agreed with nor liked.

My reasons, had I been able to formulate them into words, would have included financial considerations on top of Leif's cautionary tale. Simply put, I hadn't taken into account, before getting married, the monetary burden of supporting an unemployed wife on a low-ranking airman's salary. I assumed Alex would find a job in Ogden, but as the days wore on (and her long-distance phone bills mounted), it became clear she saw me as the sole provider. She didn't want to study nursing anymore; she expected to stay at home with a brood of babies— "additions to the family" I frankly couldn't afford!

One morning, I noticed her birth control pill case was lying slightly open on the bathroom counter. The little blister pack contained almost a full month's worth of pills, when it should have been half-empty. On the verge of a full-blown panic attack, I took a Klonopin on the spot. Then I confronted Alex: Why wasn't she taking the pills? "I forgot," she said, brushing me off like a crumb from the counter.

"Alex," I pleaded, "you *have* to be more diligent. We *cannot* get pregnant right now. Do you understand that?"

"I understand that *you* feel that way," she said. "But I'm ready now. What else am I supposed to do here all day long by myself?"

"Get a job! Help me out! Stop racking up three-hundred-dollar phone bills! You do know my monthly pay is a thousand dollars, right? That's it—that's all we have to pay for *everything* each month."

She rolled her eyes, infuriating me. I played my last card. "Take the birth control or I won't have sex with you," I warned. "We're also going to start using condoms again, regardless."

Well, the one thing Alex wanted more than a baby was for me to be loyal to her. Despite a complete lack of evidence to the contrary, she was convinced that if I didn't get sex from her at home, I would cheat on her. Jealousy ran in her blood. Reluctantly, and not a little resentfully, Alex abided by my terms. She didn't have another choice.

She also, at my insistence, started working part-time. First she said she couldn't get a job without a vehicle, so I took out a loan to buy her an older-model Pontiac Firebird (in reality, it was for me—any excuse to buy a car). That defense overturned, she took a position at Taco Bell, but quit a month or two later. In the end, it fell to me to get a second job, just to keep up with all the bills. After working eight hours at the plant, I flipped burgers at the Wendy's down the street every evening, which meant we had no time for sex anyway.

You Did It

Just as married life was taking on a more regular rhythm, my prized Mazda came due for new tires. My gear-revving games had taken a toll, and as winter dragged into a spring that never came, I needed a set with better traction in the snow. No matter how I juggled the numbers, though, I couldn't find the extra dough after groceries and bills. I decided to sell the MX-3, and let the new owner deal with the tires.

Turns out it's hard to sell a car in winter in Utah. Upon receiving a few lowball offers, I complained loudly about my plight at work. One of the guys at the plant asked me if I had full-coverage insurance on it. "Yes," I replied, "of course."

"You could report it stolen," he suggested. "Let the insurance company pay you the retail value."

I thought about it. Insurance fraud was morally dubious, no doubt, but then insurance companies have a lot of money. No one would explicitly be *hurt* by the plan, and I in turn stood to gain everything. Here's where I channeled my father's long-ago attempt to defraud the bus terminal's cash register, and made a really stupid decision. Several stupid decisions, actually, since I implicated lovely Leif as well.

Near the end of March 1993, I drove the Mazda north out of Ogden and over the county line. I ditched it in a remote field, broke the window and removed the radio (to make a "theft" seem more legitimate), and set my baby on fire. That way, there'd be no chance of repairing the car; it would have to be assessed as a total loss. I stood and watched long enough to feel the flames' warmth, then Leif, who'd followed me in his car, gave me a lift back to town. He accompanied me into the mall, where I filed my report, adrenaline still making my voice shake.

The car I set on fire to collect the insurance money.

A couple of hours later, the police showed up on my doorstep. "We found your car," the lead officer said, "and we have some questions for you."

I walked them through my "story." I'd been at the mall the whole time, I lied. "When I walked outside, the Mazda was gone."

"Really? Because we think you did it."

"And what gives you that absurd idea?"

"The can of lighter fluid with your fingerprints on it."

"Fingerprints?" I scoffed. "From a can inside a car that you told me was completely destroyed by fire?" I tried playing it tough. Really, I was scared to death.

"If you confess," they said, "we'll go easier on you than if you make us go talk to your friend."

Crap. Someone from the station at the mall remembered Leif.

They packed up and told me they'd be back after questioning him. Immediately after shutting the door, I took two Klonopin and weighed my options. Alex didn't encourage me one way or the other; she merely listened to me talk through it. Finally, wracked with guilt and determined not to let my cherished friend Leif implicate himself unnecessarily, I walked over to Leif and Syd's house and took the heat. "Just leave him out of this," I said. "It was all me."

The cops split us apart and took our statements. I was arrested and charged with arson and attempted insurance fraud. Leif got off scot-free. It's telling of my feelings for him that I was more relieved they let him go than I was upset at what happened next.

Although they'd promised to "go easy" on me, "easy" meant sitting in jail for three days until my mom could scrape together the bail money. Imagine how that phone call went: "Hi, Mom. It's me, Paul. I'm in jail for burning my car. Help?"

It was a low point in our relationship, but she managed to come through for me. In the meantime, I hired an attorney to deal with the civilian charges. "Building my case" entailed collecting character references from friends of the family who testified to my usual integrity. They wrote about knowing me in high school—how I'd been such an "upstanding young man," and they stood by that opinion. Lucky for me, the letters worked, as instead of serving five years in a Utah state prison, I got slapped with a year's probation and one hundred-fifty hours of community service. The Air Force likewise put me on probation. They further denied my next promotion to senior airman—a doubly-hard punishment, as I really could have used the pay increase.

Instead of making back my original $15,000 investment as planned, I lost everything I'd saved over two years in Germany. I sold the ruined Mazda for scrap, netting $300 total, and had to drive Alex's Pontiac to work. Somehow, I also had to find more hours in the day to make more income, as there was a bail bondsman to pay now and whopping attorney fees.[23] My wife might have loved me, but I realized I didn't love her.[24] Leif, whom I did love, didn't love me back. I felt embarrassed by what I'd done, and ashamed at how badly I embarrassed my

---

[23] Letters I wrote to my mother at this time reflect the incremental repayments I was making to her, often fifty dollars a month on a five-thousand-dollar note.

[24] Alex started asking for more and more sex during this time, too. She felt sure I was screwing one or all of the cashiers at Wendy's. To be fair, I did briefly like one of my female coworkers, but we didn't have an affair. How could we? I was either at work, or asleep, or at my other job, definitely burning the candle from both ends.

family.[25] With nowhere to go but up, I put my head down and vowed to never again cheat the system, or do things the fast and easy way. It just wasn't worth it.

Trashed It All

In late May or early June 1993, Syd called it quits with Leif and true to her word, moved back to California with their daughter. Upset, Leif began to drink more. Sensing my opening, I joined him.

One night before Leif was scheduled to move back on base, having lost his married housing allocation, Alex and I invited him over for Game Night. In private, I let Leif know Alex wanted to play strip poker. I then told Alex the same about Leif. A few cocktails in, we got down to business. By the time the three of us were naked, we were also drunk. One thing led to another, and we ended up having a three-way. Leif and I didn't actually have sex, but just seeing him naked got me very turned on. It was the best, hottest sex Alex and I had ever enjoyed. So much so, that the following morning she asked if I was gay.

"What? Why would you say that?" I demanded.

"I've never seen you so turned on."

I denied it, but she'd seen through my game. She knew my arousal was more attributable to Leif than to her. It didn't matter, though, because once Leif moved back to the dorms, I only saw him at work, and not, after that, in a social context.

---

[25] To my mom's credit, she forgave and forgot more quickly than I expected. In April 1993, she mailed me a book of poems entitled *Life Can Be Hard Sometimes, but It's Going to Be Okay*. It became my mantra for the year.

Figuring, perhaps, to "get back at me," Alex picked fights with me daily. Our biggest source of contention remained the phone. Because she still hadn't broken her long-distance telephone habit, I started taking the phone receiver with me when I left the house; that way, she couldn't run up the bill. In retaliation, she became friendly with the neighbor guy across the street. "*He* doesn't mind if I use his phone," she said— hinting "something more" may have been going on, and hoping I would be jealous. I wasn't. Whether she was sleeping with the neighbor guy or not didn't phase me. I was just thrilled to have someone else pay for her phone calls while I focused on getting us out from under our crushing financial mess.

That's not to say I gave up on the marriage. I continued to try to make it work. I began seeing a therapist weekly at the mental health clinic on base, and asked Alex if she would join me for couples counseling. She refused. The therapist upped my dosage of Klonopin and gave me some Valium as well. These effectively masked, but could not fix, my failing relationship. As a last resort, in September 1993 I called my mother. Both she and Gramaw Green knew Alex and I had been struggling. "Mom, I don't know what else to do," I said. "I've tried everything, but Alex just won't meet me halfway."

"We're coming," Mom said, meaning she and my grandmother. I don't know what she heard in my voice, but it was enough to make her drop everything and get in the car. They were worried, they later told me, that I'd do something else stupid—stupid enough to cost me my career.

I let Alex know the women were on their way. Very matter-of-factly, Alex asked me to buy her a bus ticket home. I did, no fight or argument. Before Mom and Gramaw made it halfway to Utah, Alex was on her way out. In that way, our life together ended as strangely as it had begun—at a Greyhound bus station.[26]

My family members arrived two days later. I was happy to see them, if a bit scared. I understood how things must have looked to them: like I was making poor decision after poor decision, and on the verge of screwing up irredeemably. They suggested I go to work and they would deep-clean the apartment. "You'll feel better in a tidy space," Mom assured me. "Off you go. We'll take care of it."

Well, I should have recognized their offer for what it was. With me out of the house, they could search my place and belongings for "evidence" of wrongdoing—i.e., the *reasons* I kept messing up in their eyes. In my closet, Mom found a box full of Madonna posters I'd collected over the years, plus a coffee table book that Madonna had recently published called simply, *Sex*. Along with stacks of "inappropriate" CDs, and other favorite possessions they decided I didn't need, these ended up in the garbage. "I trashed it all," Mom said, clearly triumphant. "And I don't want to hear it. It's for your own good!"

As violated as I felt, I couldn't help but marvel: *Here I am, attracted to men, and you think Madonna is the problem!*

"That woman is the devil," my mother sneered, like she could read my thoughts. Beside her, Gramaw glowered in disapproval. The lecturing continued for some time. I'd disappointed them. I wasn't living up to my potential. They were going to fix me.

---

[26] Getting divorced was so clearly the right thing to do for both of us, that neither Alex nor I contested anything. Within a few months' time, our lives were firmly our own again—or rather, mine was. Alex had gotten pregnant right away by Melissa's cousin, confirming that I'd been wise to use contraceptives. I was so relieved when she told me the baby wasn't mine; I dodged a major bullet there.

Ha. Alex was supposed to "fix" me, too.

I didn't relax until they left. Then, and only then, in the loud silence of a formerly frenetic household, did I lay down on the bed I'd last shared with my wife, and feel the weight of seven months slip off my shoulders.

Disco Ball

Thanks to Alex's and my pending divorce, I lost my off-base allotment and had to move back into the dorms. The dorm manager was a good friend of mine, and he arranged for me and Leif to become roommates. Leif was already dating another woman (a coworker of mine from Wendy's, to whom, like a perfect martyr, I'd introduced him), but I still loved getting to spend so much time with him. While Leif and this woman eventually got married, and although he and I never enjoyed another sexual encounter, he really was a solid friend, and I counted myself lucky to wake up in the same room as him for as long as it lasted.

With fewer expenses and more disposable income, I decided to trade in Alex's Pontiac Firebird for a newer, though still used, Eagle Talon. An all-around sportier vehicle, it came with all-wheel drive for the Utah snow, which I used to rationalize the otherwise unnecessary purchase. I had fun with that car—more fun, even, than the Mazda. It symbolized freedom to me, emancipation from my marriage and the dead weight of regret. I didn't know it would introduce me to my husband.

I was waxing the Talon on base one weekend, when a female airman parked her Plymouth Laser in the wash bay next to mine. I might not have noticed her, except that her Laser was a carbon copy of my Talon. Mitsubishi and Chrysler had jointly produced three nearly identical cars that year—the Mitsubishi Eclipse, the Eagle Talon, and the Plymouth Laser—giving me and this butch-presenting stranger a prominent talking point. Her name was Kelli, I learned, and she, too, loved cars. She'd just arrived at Hill from another base in the States, and like me, Hill was her second tour of duty. We became instant friends. *Lord, did you send Kelli to save me?* I wondered. *This lesbian who likes cars? Are we meant to save each other?*

The short answer? Yes.

Through Kelli, I got to know Donald, a big, tall black man and one of the first publicly "out" airmen I would meet. Donald later told me, "I knew you were gay the minute I met you," but respectfully, he never said a thing as Kelli and I started dating. He often came along on our dates, which didn't seem weird at the time, probably because both Kelli and I were pretending. One night, Donald invited us to check out a club with him in downtown Salt Lake City. "It's a dance club," he said, "popular with both straight and gay people." We thought that sounded fine, a good excuse to get off base and switch up the scenery.

As the appointed weekend drew closer, my excitement grew. What a perfect opportunity to check out, under the cover of my "straight" girlfriend, a place full of gay people! Unbeknownst to me, Donald was trying, in his infinitely compassionate way, to give me a push in the right direction. He didn't want Kelli and I to continue down a potentially harmful path.

I took an extra Klonopin before we left base, lest a panic attack ruin the evening. It was a thirty-five-minute drive to downtown, and even without traffic, it seemed to take forever. But that was just my nerves talking. I had no idea what to expect, and was afraid of being unintentionally outed. What if I somehow gave myself away? What if, like those men who catcalled me in Germany, the club patrons could "tell" I was gay?

"Bricks," appropriately housed in an old brick warehouse in Salt Lake's industrial district, was already bumping by the time we showed up. Attractive, well-dressed people—mostly male (there were *maybe* a half-dozen women in the whole club)—stood in line at the bar, crowded the dance floor, and spilled out to smoke on the patio. Mariah Carey blared from the speakers. Gel lights spun dizzyingly around the large room. Everyone was checking everyone else out, including, as we walked in, me, Donald, and Kelli. I felt equal parts empowered and exposed. Clearly, Bricks was more like a gay club where straights were welcome than the other way around, and I'd never experienced anything like it.

We had a great time dancing and drinking until the wee hours of the night. I remember thinking, *I need to come back here, but without Kelli*, then feeling bad. She was a wonderful woman, but she didn't make me feel *vital*—the way our evening at Bricks had. I'd sparkled on that dance floor: a disco ball reflecting the light of a hundred hungry pairs of eyes. I wanted to always feel that honest, that seen, that free.

I wanted to be me.

The Right Amount of Attention

"Can we go back?" I asked Donald, later that week. "Just you and me?"

He smiled at me knowingly, and promised not to tell Kelli. At least until I figured myself out.

The following Friday, I stressed over my outfit. How could I achieve the perfect medium, simultaneously blending in and standing out, to attract just the right amount of attention? I opted for an oversized long-sleeved shirt (massive on my extra small frame), tucked into jeans done up with a braided belt, tennis shoes, and a leather jacket from Wilson's (I'd recently started a new civilian job at Wilson's leather store—no more smelling like hamburgers for me).

Donald sensed my nervous energy, and advised me to "relax and go with the flow." *Easier said than done*, I thought, as at Bricks, there was no room for the old, familiar signposts of family and faith. These were uncharted waters, whose roles and rules I didn't know.

Once at the club, Donald bought me a drink, and we cruised the perimeter, soaking in the scene. It was too loud to talk, so we finished our drinks quickly, then Donald went back for a second round. While waiting for him at a hightop, I was approached by a creepy, greasy-looking guy, who reminded me of a flying monkey from *The Wizard of Oz*. I didn't want to be rude, but he couldn't take a hint, and his persistent attempts at conversation were making me uncomfortable. *Eject! Eject!* I motioned to Donald, when finally I caught sight of him again. Donald nodded, but he wasn't alone. Walking with him, straight toward me and the flying monkey, was a handsome stranger, who only had eyes for me.

Silly, Paul. You thought Donald would rescue you.

But from that moment on, I was a goner.

What tangled webs we weave, reader, believing we know what's best for ourselves, while denying our deepest desires at every turn! I was twenty-three years old and a divorcee before I could admit—just to myself—that I am gay. Should I live to see one hundred, I will have spent a quarter of my life faking it, trying to "make it," and drowning in guilt and self-hatred. By nature, fake-it-till-you-make-it is a faulty premise. None of us ever becomes anything real, satisfying, or self-actualizing by playing pretend...no matter how badly we want, or how urgently hard we try, to make a thing true.

I would not—indeed, could not—have met the love of my life, and at the same time, found actual happiness and success, if I hadn't said yes to what I knew, in my heart *and* my loins, was right for me. "Right" is not the same as easy. It would be a hard path, as painful sometimes as the lie. Overhauling your engine, after all, is time-consuming and labor-intensive. But the payoff...

Oh, the payoff.

7

Billionaire's Brat

"My name's Jeffrey." He extended a confident, wedding-ring-free hand.

I took it, feeling the strength in those fingers, and the tenderness. The whole time, I looked him in the eye. Brown eyes. Brown hair, cut so that it flopped over his forehead boyishly. He was a man, though—twenty years my senior, but didn't look it. His tailored, understated clothes, straight white teeth, and perfect skin spoke of money, but he wasn't pretentious. He was warm, smart, and ever so illogically interested in me.

"I'm Paul. Nice to meet you."

I had to look up at Jeffrey as he was an inch or two taller than me. Not muscular, but not skinny, either. He smelled of vetiver and magnolia—some kind of expensive cologne.

"Thanks for saving me from the flying monkey."

He laughed, confused but intrigued. I explained what I meant, and about a dozen other things, as he asked me question upon question. In fact, Jeffrey kept me so busy answering him that I never had a chance to return the favor. By the time Bricks closed, he knew I was an airman (and made it crystal clear that the thought of me in uniform turned him on), that I'd never dated men, and that it was my second trip ever to a gay bar. The only thing he shared about himself all night was his age.

"Thirty-two," he lied when I asked. As I would later find out,

Jeffrey was closer to forty-two; but in the gay world, age can be a deal-breaker. He would have been pleasantly surprised to learn I couldn't have cared less.

We danced until the overhead lights came on, grooving and sweating to Tina Turner and Gloria Estefan. Our bodies fit together like raindrops on a window, one caressing the other as we dripped and slipped into oblivion. At some point, I stopped drinking alcohol; Jeffrey was intoxicating enough. That he seemed to think the same of me blew my mind. Always, in the past, I'd been the one to seek approval, to chase the affections of friends, of girls, of Leif, of my family. Now, without my having to ask, Jeffrey was giving me his undivided attention. He'd trained his laser-like vision on unlikely Paul Flamer, and I, his grateful focal point, loved it.

"Do you want to go somewhere else?" he asked, as we shuffled out into the night.

"I don't know you very well," I said, suddenly shy. "Maybe another night?"

"Tomorrow?"

Donald, my steadfast friend, answered for me. "Yes. We'll be at The Sun. See you there."

"See you there," Jeffrey parroted.

My stomach tingling and my heart boom-booming, I could feel his eyes on me all the way to my car.

Long-Repressed and Primal

I had no idea, then, who the mysterious, lies-about-his-age Jeffrey was. Donald knew him—or rather, knew *of* him— since as it turned out, in certain circles Jeffrey was a celebrity. Apparently, he owned a tech company that had recently hit it big—like billionaire-status big. In 1993, I knew nothing about computers, my sum total exposure being the dot-matrix printers on base. I envisioned Jeffrey selling floppy disks and copy paper from a mall kiosk. *Good for him*, I thought, and left it at that. His financial prospects, like his age, made little difference to me. I was more concerned about what I should wear Saturday night.

All day Saturday, I fretted over seeing Jeffrey again. I couldn't wait to see him, but also, he intimidated me, in the same way the whole "gay scene" did. Everything was new to me then. I was standing in front of my wardrobe, clothes piled all over the bed, when Kelli knocked on the door. Call me a bad person, but I didn't answer. I couldn't. Not only was I a bad liar, but I hated lying, period, and I definitely couldn't tell her the truth about where I'd been the night before, or where I'd be that night. So, I avoided her. It's not like we had cell phones in the early '90s; if we didn't physically interact, I was in the clear!

Donald and I left for Salt Lake City around 8:00 p.m. Saturday night. We went to his boyfriend's house first so I could meet Orlando, who plied us with drinks and got us loosened up for the evening (a doctor, Orlando was closeted, so he didn't come out with us that night or any other). Closer to 10:30, Donald and I drove to "The Sun," short for The Sun Trapp, a lively LGBT dance club. "You're Paul?" the bouncer asked as he checked our IDs. "Jeffrey is over there," indicating a table with a clear view of the door. "He's been waiting for you since nine."

Oops.

Jeffrey recognized us right away. His face lit up—happy, probably, that we hadn't stood him up—and he waved for us to join him. We wandered over and sat down, and for the rest of the evening, we talked, drank on Jeffrey's tab, and danced any time a particularly good song played. As it had been the first time, our chemistry was palpable, but we also got to know each other better interpersonally. For example, I revealed my divorce from Alex was not quite finalized, meaning that, technically, I was still married. "Me, too!" Jeffrey said, which surprised me, since he didn't wear a ring. Evidently, his wife knew he was gay, and they planned to divorce at some point—but in the meantime, they were raising four kids together. *It must be a normal thing*, I realized, *for most gay guys to get married to, or at least date, women, while they figure their lives out.* Learning Jeffrey had a wife made me feel more at ease around him, and like less of a freak.

When The Sun announced last call, Jeffrey asked again if I wanted to go someplace else with him. "Let me ask Donald," I said. "I'm his ride."

"No problem," Donald said, once I'd pulled him aside to explain. "I can stay at Orlando's tonight, and he can drive me back to base in the morning."

"Yeah, but, is it okay?" I pressed him. "I mean, do you think I should do it?"

"You should do what you feel comfortable with," Donald advised.

"You're right. Okay. I'm going to do it!"

Donald grinned and slapped my back. "Have fun, man. And be safe, yeah?"

I rolled my eyes. If sex with Alex had taught me anything, it was "better safe than sorry."

Jeffrey walked us out to the parking lot, said goodbye to Donald, then told me to follow him in my car to Little America, an upscale hotel less than ten minutes away. On the drive there, I kept shaking my head in wonder. *Am I really doing this? Is this really happening?*

We entered the large, impressive lobby together—not holding hands, or touching in any obvious way—but still, I thought everyone could tell. And I was almost lightheaded with it, like a virgin schoolgirl up to no good. At the desk, Jeffrey got us a room, and then we were in that room, completely alone, completely infatuated.

He was gentle with me, though assertive enough to take the lead. He knew it was my first time with a man. We made out for a while, touching each other all over, until I couldn't take it anymore. Then he took me. It was Ben and Louie and Leif all over again, but infinitely *more*: more passionate, more electric, more meaningful. The sex felt amazing, but so, too, did the act of loving a man without shame.

Because Jeffrey accepted me just the way I was, I accepted myself. I accepted *us*, even before there was really an "us" of which to speak. He unleashed something in me, long-repressed and primal—a euphoria I would later try to replicate with drugs, and without much success. *This is good*, I judged. *It's good, and it's* me.

Premium Gasoline

Being with Jeffrey was like filling my tank with premium gasoline. The whole world burned cleaner and brighter in his presence, and I converted that higher octane gas into unprecedented energy and motion. Suddenly, I couldn't sit still. I wanted to spend every moment with Jeffrey. Dancing with him to "Dream Lover" by Mariah Carey. Talking to him. Exploring his body. Sleeping in his arms. Luxuriating in the perfect light of his gaze. That's how he made me feel—like I was perfect.

It killed me to have to leave him the next morning, but I was scheduled to work at Wilson's, so I dashed off with a grateful kiss and giddy smile. I thought about Jeffrey every hour of the day until we met up again, a week later, back at Brick's.

When Donald and I walked in on Friday night, there was Jeffrey—a round of drinks at the ready, a matching giddy smile on his face. We had another sublime night out, though

I noticed something interesting this time. No one approached me, when I was with Jeffrey, to interrupt. In fact, the crowd gave our whole table a wide, respectful berth. It was true, then: Jeffrey's reputation preceded him. If I was with him, then I was off-limits to everyone else.

I told Jeffrey, on this night, about my family. Everything that I'd done to make them happy, including joining the military and marrying Alex. "You know," he said, after listening attentively, "the only person you have to make happy is yourself."

"That's a great concept, Jeffrey," I conceded, "but at this point in my life, the guilt and the fear are hardwired. I can see the life I'd like to live, just like I can see it's not mine to live. My happiness doesn't matter."

He frowned. "Spend the night with me," he whispered. "Let me convince you otherwise."

I did, and it was magical. Come next morning, though, it was back to reality, and my sorry life as an airman with a second job, a mountain of debt, a pending divorce, and criminal charges.

"I wish you didn't have to leave so soon," Jeffrey said.

"Yeah, well, somebody's got to pay the bills," I sighed. Jeffrey knew everything about my situation; I'd been very open and honest with him.

"If you had more money, would that mean you could work less?"

"Sure."

"And then we could spend more time together?"

I smiled. "In another life, Jeffrey."

He thought for a moment. "I want to pay your debts off."

"Ha! I want you to, too," I joked, shaking my head.

"No, really. Will you let me?"

I stopped buttoning my shirt to look at him. "You're being serious."

"I am."

"I could never."

"Couldn't you, though? The money's not an issue for me, Paul. I have plenty of money. What I don't have is another you."

I was shocked, but after we talked it through, I agreed that being debt-free would reduce my stress and workload significantly. Without another word, Jeffrey opened his wallet and gave me $2,000 cash—more money than I made in a month. In a daze, I thanked him and drove to the mall, where I quit my job at Wilson's and didn't look back.

Jeffrey's gift covered the balance of my attorney fees, an outstanding phone bill, and several car payments. Without these anvils hanging over my head, I was free to see Jeffrey more often. Most of the time we met in Salt Lake City, though once I invited him back to my dorm room (Leif had since moved out, so I had the room to myself). I loved watching his fancy Mercedes 600 SEL V-12 pull into an on-base parking spot between the rest of the airmen's beaters. Jeffrey and I were actually having sex in my room when Kelli tried to beat the door down. "I know you're in there, Flamer!" I broke up with her later that night, never admitting to her I was gay, but believing I was doing her a favor.

From there on out, Jeffrey and I were "unofficially-officially" dating.

Dylan

"So, there are some things you need to know if we're going to be together," Jeffrey told me, once we'd decided to become boyfriends. I already knew about his wife and kids. That relationship was strategic, not romantic, so I could deal.

"But, I also have an ex, Brett, who technically still lives with me," Jeffrey confessed, sending my heart into my stomach. Apparently, Jeffrey lived apart from his wife Amelia,[27] in a small house in Orem (just south of Salt Lake City), and while he and Brett were no longer an item, Brett had yet to move back to Australia. "Right after Christmas," Jeffrey promised, "I'll tell him he needs to leave. Okay?"

This revelation was harder to swallow, but I chastised myself: *You have no point of reference for gay relationships, Paul. It might be totally normal for a man and his ex to live together. Give Jeffrey the benefit of the doubt.*

"Okay," I consented.

I had no reason to doubt Jeffrey anyway, since for the most part, we went everywhere as a couple. He introduced me to his friends, including his hairdresser and confidante Ruth (another person who watched me and reported back to Jeffrey). Everyone was nice to and accepting of me. He also took me shopping, a *lot*. I still didn't know the full extent of Jeffrey's wealth, but I was happy to let him pay when we went out, and to buy me little gifts here and there, as it seemed to bring him as much joy as it did me. One of the first things he bought me was a pair of picture frames from OC Tanner, a high-end jewelry store in Salt Lake. They were green leather and chrome silver, respectively, and cost the equivalent of a car payment. "I couldn't," I again protested.

---

[27] Jeffrey and Amelia were living apart then—but prior to their separation, Jeffrey had actually invited the boyfriend before Brett to move in with himself and Amelia! She and the kids lived upstairs, while Jeffrey and his boyfriend Mitch lived downstairs. I could hardly believe the audacity, until Jeffrey then did the same thing with me—inviting me to stay over with him while Brett still lived at the house in Orem.

"Hush. I want to," Jeffrey insisted.

The staff, who knew him and called him by his first name, wrapped the frames up for me beautifully. I put photos of Jeffrey in both of them, where they remain to this day.

Sometime in late Fall 1993, Jeffrey asked me to come stay at his house in Orem. It was a milestone for us, as we'd been meeting almost exclusively in hotels. Exiting the freeway to get to his place, I passed a warehouse with the name of his company emblazoned on it in block print. The building was probably 10,000 square feet, and I remember thinking, *No wonder he can throw cash around and pay for dinners and drive a Mercedes like it's nothing.* His house, on the other hand, was comparatively modest: three-bedrooms, with a two-car garage and swimming pool.

When I mentioned seeing the building to Jeffrey, he laughed, and said, "Oh, that's just the warehouse for shipping products." He then opened the blinds on the large bay window in the living room, and pointed to a group of multi-story buildings in a sprawling industrial complex. "All of that is my company."

"Whoa!" I enthused. It was impressive, on a scale I couldn't really grasp, but Jeffrey's holdings didn't impact my feelings for him.

I only visited Jeffrey at his house in Orem on weekends when Brett wasn't in town. If Brett was home, we stayed at a hotel, until that routine turned wearisome. Six months later, in May 1994, Jeffrey would get us an apartment halfway between Hill Air Force Base and Orem, in the bedroom community of Bountiful, Utah. "It won't cost any more than paying for all those hotels," he half-teased, half-soothed me. "Besides, it's safer." He meant safer for me, as Department of Defense Directive 1304.26, otherwise known as Don't Ask, Don't Tell, had just been issued on December 21, 1993. For the same reason, Jeffrey had recently purchased me a cell phone, so we could talk any time without restrictions, or fear of being monitored (it was also a way for him to keep tabs on me at all times).

"I am very happy I met you, Paul," Jeffrey wrote in a letter from December '93. "It has made a huge difference in the way I feel about myself and about life right now…I enjoy life now, mostly because I am always looking forward to seeing you the next time." I felt the same—happier in general, with a more positive outlook on life than perhaps ever before.

It seemed like everything was going well for us—fast, but well—when Christmas rolled around, and with it, the deadline for Jeffrey to keep his promise. But he didn't ask Brett to leave, at least not as quickly as I would have liked. Instead, he kept making excuses. "It's Brett's birthday soon," he told me. "I can't ask him to leave on his birthday." There was always another reason why the moment was inopportune, and Brett's "eviction" dragged well into 1994. While I cared for Jeffrey (maybe even loved him), I couldn't sit at home and wait, so I started going to the gay bars again with Donald.

One night, I met a man named Dylan through a mutual friend. Dylan was Hispanic-looking (though he was adopted, so who knows?) and very cute, just a few years younger than me. We flirted every time we saw each other, until eventually we hooked up in the spring. So smitten was I by Dylan that I told him I would leave Jeffrey for him. "Don't be stupid," Dylan admonished me. "You have a good thing going with Jeffrey." I realized he was right, and overcome with guilt, I told Jeffrey about Dylan the next morning.

"How could you?" Jeffrey wanted to know. He was mad—but such were the consequences of his own actions. He'd set our crooked love triangle up in a way that was shady from the beginning. Once Brett was gone, he'd expect me to be his whole life, like he owned me.

"Why not?" I challenged. "You have your side piece Brett. It's only fair. Or can't I have my cake and eat it, too?" Then, inspired by the memory of me, Leif, and Alex, I threw out: "Maybe you, me, and Dylan could have a three-way?"

Jeffrey didn't seem thrilled by the idea, but agreed to try it.

Later that week, Dylan met Jeffrey and me at the Bountiful apartment. I skipped ahead to "That's the Way Love Goes" in the CD player to set the mood. Jeffrey tried his hardest, but Dylan wasn't into him, and after a time, Jeffrey left crying. I apologized to Dylan, saw him out, and said I'd call him soon. We never talked again, though. Every time I called him, Dylan wouldn't answer or return my messages. I suspected Jeffrey had paid him to disappear, but didn't confirm this suspicion until recently, when Dylan alluded to as much after we reconnected on Facebook.

The Billionaire's Brat

Jeffrey tried to make it up to me—or maybe "distract me" is the better phrase here—with beautiful words. Were they heartfelt? Empty? I didn't know. And he kept buying me ever more elaborate gifts. In early 1994, he mailed me a list of "plusses and minuses" for "who he was," that attempted to explain away his shortcomings and apologize for them all at the same time. On the "minus" side, he wrote: "I am not 23. In fact, I am what some people in their twenties would consider old." On the "plus" side, though: "I am willing to bend until it hurts."

He put me on his company's payroll, as a way to legitimize the extra spending money he'd started funneling in my direction. I was listed on the books as a "mechanic," which meant I spent weekends cleaning and detailing his personal vehicles. It made me happy to give something back to Jeffrey in return for him always helping me out.

One weekend, he told me the new house he'd been building just a few blocks away from his current house was ready; would I help him move the cars over there? He drove his Mercedes SL, and I grudgingly followed in Brett's matching SL. I didn't know anything about the new house except that it was "bigger," which it turned out was putting it mildly. Soon, we came to a tall brick fence that seemed to go on forever. I was so in awe of the enormous wrought iron gates that I wasn't watching where I was going and almost rear-ended Jeffrey, who'd stopped to wait for the gates to open. Thank goodness Mercedes makes brakes that work well even in the snow. A long, tree-lined driveway led up to a seven-car garage, and a monster 15,000-square-foot house—the Orem Manor, we called it—came into view.[28] Suddenly, everything I thought I knew or had assumed about Jeffrey seemed like child's play. He wasn't just rich. He was World's-Top-Executives Rich.

"Are you kidding me?" I asked Jeffrey, once we'd parked on a behemoth stone pad.

---

[28] At the same time, Jeffrey's ex-wife Amelia was building her own 15,000-square-foot mansion across town. They both lived in Orem, albeit as far apart as possible, so they could share the kids, who alternated holidays with Mom and Dad. Using the four hundred million dollars she'd won in their divorce settlement, Amelia hired the same person who designed the Orem Manor to design her house, which ended up being done in a totally different style. If you ask me, what "bad blood" may have existed between Jeffrey and Amelia was more the product of heartache than hate. Amelia loved Jeffrey. She was devastated when he left her, even though his being gay had nothing to do with her. I mean, it's not like she did anything "wrong." Because of that, she never really got over him. Jeffrey honored her pain by not mixing his worlds. As a result, I never spent any time with Amelia, except in passing.

"No. Would you like to take the tour?"

I accepted his outstretched hand. "Sure, but don't get too far ahead of me. I could get lost in there."

Inside, the sheer size of the space, not to mention the decadence of the fittings and design, blew me away. The hallways split into endless small corridors. Rooms opened up into extra, hidden rooms. *All this for one person?* I thought.

But it wasn't just for Jeffrey; it was for Brett, too, and also for me, as I'd start spending the occasional evening here. And I would get used to it more quickly than I'd have believed. Soon, it would feel comfortable—even cozy. I'd grow accustomed to that level of wealth, that lifestyle, as I unwittingly became the billionaire's brat.

Racking up as many miles as I did driving my used Eagle Talon back and forth between base and the Orem Manor, it didn't surprise me when the check engine light came on. Rather than pay to fix the first in what was sure to be a line of inevitable car faults and failures, Jeffrey offered to buy me a new car—"Any kind you want, Paul." In April 1994, I found a '93 Mitsubishi 3000 GT (the last one on the lot, since the '94 models had already arrived) at a dealership near base, and after negotiating $4,000 off the price tag, wrote a check for the full amount. "It's a felony to bounce a check this large," the skeptical general manager reminded me. He must never have seen a check for $40,000.

"Oh, it won't bounce," I assured him. Jeffrey had already wired me the money. "Plus, I'm in the military. If you need to find me, it won't be hard."

I drove my latest baby off the lot and straight to Salt Lake City, where Janet Jackson was performing that night at the Delta Center. The album she released the year before, titled simply *janet.,* was one of my favorites.

Someone once said, "If money can fix it, it's not a problem," a sentiment that really only applies to the extraordinarily wealthy. When you're in debt, as I was before meeting Jeffrey (and would be again, eventually), every little "problem" feels huge and insurmountable, as there is no money to throw at a thing and make it go away. Rather, the problems pile up, and in my case, stress and anxiety add to them. If you're then further dealing with some inner turmoil—for example, repressing the fact that you're gay—it can actually feel like the world is ending. Who knows what would have happened had I not met Jeffrey? Who knows what life would be like were we still together today?

That said, Jeffrey did solve a lot of my problems with money, and he fixed some of the deeper ones, too. In choosing me, and choosing to live "out and proud" with me, he healed what his bank account couldn't have made a dent in. He took Broken Paul, reeling from a rash of bad decisions, and made me feel wanted; sexual; seen. He released me from the stocks of mental and social bondage (not the sexy-fun kind!) I'd volunteered my head and hands for, and he told me to stand up, claim my worth, and own my joy. I may have become a billionaire's brat, but I chose Jeffrey, like he chose me. Like you must choose the people, the ideas, and the love you want in your life.

You should be able to love and trust your family of origin: your parents, your grandparents, your siblings, if applicable. They've known you from the beginning, and that's a very valuable metric. If it makes them think they also know what's best for you, however, and they start rummaging through and throwing away your prized collection of Madonna paraphernalia—well, just understand there's more than one way to be. Remaining a prisoner does no one any good. So stand up, claim your worth, and own your joy—and don't be afraid, like me in the next chapter, to let your "freak flag fly" when life calls for it!

8

Living Large

Around the time I met Dylan, when I was frequenting the gay clubs again, I also became intimate with Salt Lake City's drag scene. Drag queens were fixtures at most gay clubs in the 1990s, and the more of them I saw, the more I started to think, *Hey, I could do that.* Often, these queens had big, muscular physiques that they tried to correct for with corsets and the precursors to Spanx, and while some of them did look quite beautiful, they didn't exactly look feminine. I, on the other hand, with my tall, slender frame and high cheekbones, had a naturally feminine appearance. What had always worked against me in my youth played heavily to my advantage as a would-be drag queen.

Autumn, one of the first queens I befriended (and the person who'd introduced me to Dylan, initially), was actually intersex, born partially both sexes. She didn't just dress up in women's clothes at night; she lived as a woman full-time, though she'd not yet had sex-reassignment surgery. As Autumn and I got to know each other, she helped me find my footing in the drag world, taking me shopping for outfits and wigs and teaching me how to do my make-up. I never did become proficient at makeup application, and always asked another drag queen to lend me a hand, but beyond that, I made for a passable woman, I thought. At no point did I believe I was, or want to be, trans;

rather, becoming "Tiffany" (the drag name I chose for myself, in honor of the luxury goods company Tiffany & Co.) was an opportunity, for an occasional evening, to be someone else entirely. I could forget about Paul and all of his present-day worries (chief among them, a boyfriend who wouldn't break up with his ex), not to mention his baggage (even after I was out, I would spend years unpacking the trauma of repressing my sexuality), and just have fun. It was a healthier, more cathartic version of the "play-pretend" life I'd led for so long.

My earliest foray into the drag queen scene: Tiffany.

Jeffrey wasn't necessarily "into" Tiffany like he was Paul, but he didn't stop me from performing, either. Drag queens are known for dancing and lip-syncing to popular songs that have become, over time, gay anthems—numbers like "I'm Coming Out" by Diana Ross. That was my song of choice, anyway, when I performed, which wasn't often. While I was proud to show up in my drag queen attire, I didn't like the potential for criticism and judgment that performing ushered in. Better to be the "hot bitch" (yes, Tiffany was a total bitch—another reason I loved her so much) and the envy of my bulkier, more masculine peers, than a prospective laughingstock.

Ironically, I was forced to invent another woman around this same time, one who would never actually exist, to placate my overly involved family. Ever since Alex and I had ended things, Mom had continued to worry about me, asking in every letter and on every phone call if I'd met someone new yet. I couldn't tell her about Jeffrey, so I started telling her about "Brenda," a complete fabrication of a woman based on Jeffrey. "She likes cars," I told my mother, "so that's really awesome, and she has a great job in the computer industry. She's also super Christian," I lied, to appease her, though Jeffrey, like the majority of Utahans, was Mormon (by that time, however, he was non-practicing[29]). When Mom started pressing me for photos of Brenda, one of Jeffrey's friends named Pam agreed to take a few staged pictures with me. We even took one in front of the Mitsubishi 3000 GT that "she" had bought for me. I sent these to Mom, and they satisfied her curiosity, while also "proving" that I wasn't making her up.

This gem is the photo of "Brenda" I sent to my mother to
convince her that I was dating a nice Christian girl,
when in fact I was dating Jeffrey.

---

[29]   Jeffrey ultimately left the Church of Latter-Day Saints because of their stance on homosexuality. He actually had the church remove his name from LDS records—a serious form of ex-communication.

As 1994 went on, and the end of my time in the military drew near, Brenda became the perfect excuse for staying in Utah indefinitely. Mom was concerned (and rightfully so) that without the structure and discipline of the Air Force, I would again lose my guiding purpose, and fall prey to a new round of dead-end jobs—or worse, do nothing at all and rely on "Brenda" to take care of me. That's exactly what I planned to do, of course—move in with Jeffrey and become his spoiled boy toy—but Mom couldn't know that. So I told her that while I would be moving in with Brenda, I also had some good job prospects lined up. "Really, Mom, you don't have to worry. I've turned my life around and everything's great!" She wanted to meet Brenda, but I successfully parried with, "Oh, she travels so much on business. We'll come to you instead, at our next opportunity. Promise."

I make it sound easy, but lying to my family really ate me up inside. I wanted them to know the real Paul, and I would have loved for them to meet Jeffrey, but I was still so scared that what he and I were doing was wrong. It's hard to explain how a thing can feel so right, and so intrinsically bad, at the same time, but that's how it goes when you're taught to hate homosexuals, only to realize down the road that you are one. Many gay people of my generation, and even the ones who followed (though from the outside looking in, at least, it seems to have been easier for them), never could figure out how to reconcile these two truths. So many of my friends in the community either lived "secret" lives the whole time, or if they didn't die of AIDS, killed themselves. I didn't want to keep living a lie, but I didn't think I could handle the shame of being out, either.

Most of the time, I coped by drinking excessive amounts of alcohol, the only drug I could legally consume while in the military. I depended on booze—and Tiffany—to see me through the rest of my enlistment, at which point the next chapter of my life would begin.

My Friend, Paul

In July 1994, I received an honorable discharge from the United States Air Force. Jeffrey threw me a joint birthday-slash-getting-out-of-the-military party in August, at the Orem Manor, and dozens of our friends attended. The drag queens gifted me costume jewelry, high-heeled shoes, and a tiara, and even put on a small drag show to entertain the rest of the guests. I have fond memories and lots of pictures of this night, some of which even show Brett and me together, almost a whole year after Jeffrey said he would kick him out. Brett continued to hang around, despite it being obvious that Jeffrey and I were together, so reluctant was he to give up his posh (courtesy of Jeffrey) lifestyle. It's probably the same reason I tolerated Brett as long as I did—one can put up with a lot when they are living like a billionaire.

Now that I didn't have to stay on base anymore, there was no reason to keep the Bountiful apartment, or for me to live any further north than Salt Lake City. Jeffrey decided to buy a house for me in town—"Just until Brett heads back to Australia," he said—and wowed me with a five-bedroom, 3,000-square-foot house in Cottonwood Heights. It wasn't near as big as the Orem Manor, of course, but it was still the largest house I had ever lived in. Jeffrey then gave me an American Express Platinum card that was in my name but linked to his account. We also opened a joint checking account. In all our years together, I never received or saw a single statement for either account. Being with Jeffrey meant not having to pay for anything anymore, ever—and that's just how it was.

I'd like to say the money never went to my head; that I remained, at the core of me, a hard-working son from the Valley.[30] Alas, money skews your perception, and what may seem ridiculous or extraordinary to the average person became my everyday way of life. For example, we started traveling a lot, to cities and countries I'd never been to, sometimes on private jets, always first-class.[31] Wherever we landed, we had drivers to drop us off at our thousand-dollar-a-night suites. People never

[30] In all honesty, I could never fully forget where I came from, as it was Summer 1994 when my community service hours (the restitution I'd been ordered for attempted insurance fraud) came due. I was assigned to stock bottles in Utah's state-owned liquor stores, which I did twenty hours a week until I'd fulfilled the terms of my sentence. For one grown used to not working, four hours per day was a lot. The only thing that made it bearable was showing up, to the envy of the other store clerks, in the Dodge Viper I'd bought on a trip with Jeffrey to Santa Monica. I later crashed the Viper into a light pole, paid thirty thousand dollars to repair it, sold it, and got something else.

[31] One of the most memorable trips we took was to Hawaii in 1995. With Jeffrey's ex Brett still in the picture, it was easier for us to leave Salt Lake City if we wanted to have uninterrupted time together. While in Hawaii, Jeffrey let me rent a different sports car every day. I variously drove a Lotus Turbo Esprit, a Corvette, and a Ferrari, which is funny, because the roads in Hawaii aren't very long, so how fast can you really get going there? Anyway, on the day I had the Ferrari, I drove to the US Air Force Base on Hawaii to see an old friend. Sergeant Wally, my former supervisor in Germany, was then stationed in Hawaii, and I got a kick out of showing up behind the wheel of that car. He didn't know (and I didn't tell him!) that it was a rental—I wanted to impress him. "Hop in," I said. "Let's go for a spin!" It was great to see him again, as he was the one responsible for introducing me to German and Italian cars.

harassed us, or discriminated against us for being gay—Jeffrey's money (and by extension, power) spoke louder than their bias. Even when we went out in Salt Lake City, that was true. Most Salt Lakers knew Jeffrey or his company by name; he was commonly recognized in line at the grocery store. Almost as often, the fan would turn to me and ask, "Is this your son?" as I was only four years older than Jeffrey's oldest child. "No," Jeffrey would say, "this is my friend, Paul."

I was always self-conscious of my big nose, which you can see in this "modeling" picture I had taken circa 1992. Between that and my acne, other kids used to make fun of me. After I met Jeffrey, he paid for my rhinoplasty, and they just shaved the hump off.

I met many of Jeffrey's business partners, employees, and other friends this way. Two of them, Tony and Hal, were flight attendants for two different airlines, and as gay and well-traveled as we were, they became our double-date buddies. We went to dinner, shows, and clubbing all the time, and even took a weekend trip together to Beverly Hills. We flew first-class, enjoyed limousine service all weekend, and stayed at the Beverly Wilshire hotel, which as its website proclaims, "is a landmark of history and glamour just steps from Rodeo Drive." It was my first time to the area, and as surreal an experience as they come—a definite *Pretty Woman* moment for me. We dined at the best restaurants, shopped the chicest boutiques, and partied at LA's hottest clubs. Not only did I hope to live in Beverly Hills someday, I decided to change my drag name to Vivian, after Julia Roberts's *Pretty Woman* character.

As it turned out, even when we weren't together, Tony and Hal were watching me. After the whole Dylan fiasco, Jeffrey had asked them to be his extra sets of eyes, so that any time he was away, he could know what I was up to. Mostly what I was "up to" was drag. In the wake of New York's Club Kid movement, the scene in Salt Lake was growing, and I loved it. Compared to the costumes that the new wave was beginning to wear, I looked plain, so I upped my game. Eventually, I dressed in crazy outfits whether I was going out as Vivian or not. I met a promoter at gay club Vortex, who was also an up-and-coming clothing designer named Jared Gold, and I hired him to make custom clothes for me, both for daywear and for Vivian. My first drag friend Autumn and I grew so close during this time that she started staying at the Cottonwood Heights house with me regularly. Although all she ever did was my makeup, it made Jeffrey uncomfortable to know she was always around, and I'm sure he took her aside to explain his "rules" for her. This is when I learned how "trapped" Autumn felt in her intersex body, and how badly she wished to have surgery—if it wasn't so expensive.

"How expensive are we talking?" I asked.

"Thirty thousand dollars," Autumn said, making a face.

I considered her plight. While thirty large was a lot of money for most folks, Jeffrey had dropped more than that on my Mitsubishi less than six months after meeting me. And a car, while fun, was hardly life-changing, the way surgery would be for Autumn. Her presence may have threatened Jeffrey, but he still cared about her wellbeing, and I thought maybe I could convince him to help her out.

"Let me talk to Jeffrey," I offered.

It wasn't an inconsequential sum, even for him, but once he understood how much Autumn meant to me, he said he would cover her surgery using the money I'd been "banking" on his payroll. He did warn me to be careful of who I befriended in the future: "When you have money," he said, "people will pretend to be your friends, just so they can take advantage of your kindness and generosity." That wasn't the case with Autumn,[32] but it would be true of certain "friends" I made in the future. Nevertheless, his "warnings" irritated me, as they reminded me of the stepfather who'd organized his life around controlling mine.

One night, Autumn and I were out at a club. M People's "Moving on Up" was playing when this gorgeous, very well-dressed woman walked over and introduced herself to me. When she told me her name was Anastasia, I noticed her accent, and asked her where she was from. "Australia," she answered.

---

[32] Over the years, Autumn and I lost touch, but she reached out recently on LinkedIn to thank me, and let me know how much the surgery had changed her life for the better. She's currently married and living as a beautiful woman in a different country! Jeffrey and I would repeat this gesture the following year for a trans drag queen named Vanessa. I was and am very happy to have been able to help them, and only wish that my own life could have been so easily rectified with money.

"Oh, I know someone from Australia," I said. "His name is Brett."

"But I'm here visiting a Brett!" she said. She pointed across the club, and sure enough, there was Brett, Jeffrey's ex who refused to die.

Brett realized who Anastasia was talking to and quickly intervened—but not before Anastasia had spilled his secret. Apparently, Brett's Australian boyfriend was in town, and he'd brought Anastasia along with him as his beard, meaning Jeffrey wasn't the only knight on this chessboard with two boyfriends. "Of all the people you could have chatted with," Brett later chided Anastasia, "why in the world did it have to be Paul?"

She was just drawn to fabulousness, I guess.

I don't know how it all went down between Jeffrey and Brett (I wasn't going to be the one to rat Brett out to Jeffrey), but somehow Jeffrey found out about Brett's lover. The next thing I knew, Brett had packed his bags and moved back to Oz, at long last leaving Jeffrey all to myself.

Get the Party Started

Sometime in November 1994, Jeffrey surprised me with a trip to Las Vegas. Tony and Hal came with us, as well as another mutual friend, Larry, and Larry's boyfriend of the moment. Larry's family had made their money in grocery stores; he and Jeffrey met through business.

The highlight of the trip, for me, was getting to see my idol, RuPaul, in concert at the Sahara Hotel and Casino. I looked up to RuPaul—a black man dressed as a beautiful woman—for several reasons, but mainly because he preached self-love and acceptance, a message I was still trying to assimilate. "If you can't love yourself, how in the hell you gonna love somebody else?" RuPaul was fond of saying. His debut album *Supermodel of the World*, released in 1993, was everything I wanted to be: damn proud, and damn good at prancing!

While we were getting ready for the concert, Jeffrey told me he had another surprise for me. "Something to get the party started," he said, waving a plastic baggie of ecstasy pills in my direction.

I'd never done drugs, first because of Gramaw Green's insistence that they would kill me, and later because I was subject to random urine tests in the Air Force. Now that I couldn't be "caught" and dishonorably discharged, and now that I had an experienced guide (I hoped) to lead me safely through the experience (one who promised that if I didn't like it, I never had to do it again), I was out of excuses. Gramaw was the angel on one shoulder, whispering premonitions of my death; Jeffrey was the devil on the other, reassuring me everything would be fine.

Because we'd been drinking all day, and because there was a roomful of men telling me we were all in it together, I listened to the devil. Half a pill, and half an hour later, I woke up in heaven.

Ecstasy steals over you like a warm, fuzzy blanket. It's like crawling into bed with a lover, only the world is your lover, since on ecstasy, the whole world is love. Everybody loves you, you love everybody, you want them to touch you, and you want to touch them. I wasn't out to my family because I wanted their love and acceptance, but when I was high, I realized, I didn't need their approval. Love and acceptance flowed to me in pastel rivers from every direction, short-circuiting the part of my brain that still resisted, still doubted, still feared. *My God*, I thought. *Everything I've ever wanted is available, at any time, in teensy tiny pill form. This is amazing!*

Then: *When can we do it again?*

The thing about ecstasy, and all drugs, really, is that the first time is typically the best time. You can take the drug a million more times, and in ever higher doses, and never achieve a high like your initial high—though the memory of it keeps you trying. I would find the same to be true of cocaine, GHB, heroin, and the myriad other drugs I snorted or swallowed over the next decade. It's true what they say—"X" and ex-boyfriends are the best gateway drugs. I often wonder if Jeffrey would take this night back if he could.

At any rate: RuPaul was amazing. His show was amazing. The night was amazing. Jeffrey was amazing. I acted more open and loving toward him than my normally inhibited, sober self ever did.[33] I stopped obsessing every waking moment over what I looked like, what people thought of me, and who could tell I was gay. I simply reveled in being alive, and being in love.

The next day, Jeffrey cautioned me against making any major decisions. "The caveat to taking ecstasy," he explained, "is that what goes up, must come down, and while your serotonin levels are re-stabilizing, it's important not to do anything drastic." He was right: For two days, I was a crying, emotional mess. But, at least in the beginning, the unavoidable low wasn't enough to put me off the high. I was only twenty-four, after all—young enough yet to feel invincible.

---

[33] Ecstasy, or MDMA, was developed by a German pharmaceutical company in 1912. It gained a small following among psychiatrists beginning in the late 1970s, who found the drug enhanced communication in patient sessions by reducing anxiety and encouraging a sense of intimacy. That's what ecstasy does: It knocks down psychic barriers, making you feel safe, warm, loved.

Love Will Follow

Ecstasy was so much better, so much more effective than alcohol alone at numbing the pain, that I quickly progressed to weekly use. Why go without the drug when it was so readily available, and with Jeffrey's means at my disposal, so endlessly affordable? I had no job, and nothing I was responsible for, which meant there were no (immediate) repercussions. Instead, every Friday and Saturday night for the next three years, I treated partying like it *was* my job, eventually styling myself as an ecstasy "connoisseur."

Like a wine connoisseur, I learned everything there was to know about ecstasy: the different types, their varying ingredients and effects, how long the high specific to each pill would last. To be fair, this was possible because MDMA was more controlled, and therefore more uniform, back then; it wasn't the street drug of today, which might be cut with anything. Most of what I read during these pre-internet days came from a 1995 book entitled *Ecstasy and the Dance Culture.* Once I mastered X, I moved on to cocaine, which allowed me to combine the warming euphoria of ecstasy with the soporific effects of alcohol and not get sleepy, so I could stay up all night and continue to have a good time.

I shared the wealth, of course, often inviting strangers from the bar back to the Cottonwood Heights house after the clubs closed, just to be known as the hostess with the mostest, so dearly did I love being the center of attention. When Jeffrey complained, I blamed Paul's bad behavior on Vivian—*she* was the one acting out, not me. These parties made me popular in our little group, a status I'd never been blessed with before. So what if I was buying their affections with drugs? They loved it, and they seemed to love me.

What experimenting with drugs and my alter-egos Tiffany and Vivian taught me was that by changing something about myself—manipulating my body chemistry, or donning a wig—I could temporarily find reprieve from my suffering, because when I used these substances, or became these people, I no longer had to be Paul. The problem was that when the high wore off, or the fake eyelashes came off, Paul was still there, along with all the pain, now intensified, that he'd been ignoring. I was tricking out my car to improve its aesthetics and its performance, but deviating too far from the manufacturer's original factory specifications, and causing far more issues than I was addressing. The worst one would be failing to come out to my father while I still had the chance.

It's okay to explore, to play around, to have new experiences, and to try on different personas as you figure out who you are and who you want to be. At the end of the day, though, whoever you've decided that person is—you've got to love them, so that as RuPaul says, you can love other people. I didn't love myself yet, not at this point (it would take almost fifteen more years), but I made it there eventually, and you will, too. In the meantime, if you need to "modify your ride" in order to embrace your body, your sexuality, or some other aspect of the self, then do it. Have fun. Just make sure that, in the words of the immortal Aretha Franklin, you R-E-S-P-E-C-T yourself along the way. Love will follow.

9

Time to Come Out

Armed with a new human shield (Jeffrey) and a new coping mechanism (ecstasy)—just in case they said *fuck you*—I finally decided it was time to come out to my family. The very thought of coming clean still gave me so much anxiety, however, that at Jeffrey's suggestion, I started seeing a therapist, who added antidepressants to my Klonopin/Valium regimen. In November 1994, this therapist helped me write a letter to my mother, in which I told her I was gay and in love with a man. The response I received crushed me.

"Your revelation last night is the saddest thing I have ever experienced," Mom wrote in her reply. "You have chosen a road of destruction and death and loneliness. … I will not think about you, as seeing you in bed with a man makes me vomit. Seeing you dying of AIDS,[34] alone, homeless, makes me cry." As

---

[34] Again, the AIDS crisis was peaking in the mid-1990s. According to hiv.gov, in 1994 AIDS became "the leading cause of death for all Americans ages 25 to 44" (accessed 9 March 2020). Let me repeat that: *all* Americans; not just gay ones. Back then, AIDS was a death sentence, and the mere thought of it struck fear into the hearts of everyone, but especially mothers. I'm not trying to minimize what she said—it was hurtful and wrong—but I can acknowledge that it came from a place of concern, based on the information she had at

if these damning projections weren't enough, she then signed her letter with a "sad face" and a drawing of a knife piercing a broken heart.

My mother's words confirmed everything I'd been afraid of, and then some. Her rejection was ten times stronger, and infinitely more painful, than I'd steeled myself for, and this wound would take years to scab over. I have my therapist to thank for keeping me level-headed enough not to react more dramatically, and instead send this simple reply, sparking a chain of letters back and forth through which both Mom and I got to have our full say.

"I've never been thrilled with the feelings I've had for the past 24 years, either," I admitted to her the next week. "But should I live the rest of my life fighting myself because society says homosexuality is not normal? Whose job is it to decide what's normal and what isn't?" Calling on my last dregs of human decency, I mailed her a Christmas gift along with this letter.

Upon receipt of it, she wrote back: "I know what you are doing to earn money to spend on expensive things [implying that I was prostituting myself to Jeffrey]. ... I do not want to profit from your misfortune." She vowed to return my gift for money, which she said she planned to spend on "gifts for a poor family." She also made it clear she considered ours a "poor family" this year, and I was not to contact my brother Peter or my sister Joy, as they, too, had been "devastated" by my news and did not want anything to do with me. The final touch was the mustard seed she included, a reference to Matthew 17:20: "For I assure you: If you have faith the size of a mustard seed,

---

the time, and the things her family and church had taught her to believe.

you will tell this mountain, 'Move from here to there,' and it will move. Nothing will be impossible for you."

In other words, if I would only *decide* to be straight, I could be. Mine was a lifestyle choice she condemned.

So much for John 8:32: "The truth shall set you free."

While it was the response I'd been expecting, it tore me in two to lose Mom's love—to find out, once and for all, that it was not unconditional.[35] I ran to my boyfriend, Jeffrey, and my girlfriend, X, for reassurance, then jumped into the deep end when no one was looking. I invited my cousins from Dallas, Isabella and Natasha, to fly up to Salt Lake, and convinced Isabella to carry a hundred ecstasy tablets onto the plane in the cups of her bra. It was at one of the parties I threw around this time when I met college roommates Eric and Bryce, Eric's blonde friend Elizabeth (who wore black patent leather body suits), and Bryce's friend Carla (a 5'9" brunette with curly hair

---

[35] Mom sent one more letter, at New Year's, that attempted to blunt the knife edge of her previous two letters: "All I have ever wanted for you children is the best life has to offer," she wrote. "I now realize that the best doesn't necessarily include the biggest house and the fanciest car ... the best is living in peace with yourselves. ... Don't look for happiness from someone else. Love yourself first. You are made in the image and likeness of God, remember that always. You were conceived in love. You are still loved." I wished she'd been able to articulate this from the get-go, because for me, the damage was already done. I would read and re-read her original letters and cry at how horrible they made me feel. Today, after years of therapy, I feel a detachment when I read them. I understand where she was in her own journey at that time, and why she wrote the cruel words she did. It's what happened, not what's happening. I know my mother loved me then, and loves me now.

and a taste for crystal meth)—four new friends who would play key roles in my life down the road.

Perpetually under the influence of drugs, and the friends those drugs won me, I became a worse brat than ever. While Jeffrey sympathized with my pain, he could only tolerate so many tantrums, and in February 1995, he left this note on my bed at the Cottonwood Heights house: "I want you to know that I am really concerned for you and what you are doing with your life, Paul. ... The people you like to talk to and play with are not people who will build you up or help you succeed. They are people who use other people until there is no more to use."

He continued: "You are not like them. Not yet, anyway. Please wake up and look at what you are doing to yourself."

When nothing about my behavior changed, Jeffrey staged an intervention (disguised as a trip around the world) that allowed him to remove me cold turkey from the club scene and control with whom and what I interacted. "We're going to Mardi Gras," he told me. "Pack your bags. We leave on Monday."

A Drag Queen Named Paris

I associated Mardi Gras with Fat Tuesday and New Orleans, but no: Jeffrey meant Mardi Gras Sydney. In the 1990s, Australia had the largest Mardi Gras party in the world, and it catered, at a time when pretty much no one else did, to the LGBT community. Late in February, we caught a sixteen-hour, first-class flight to Sydney. I was nervous about the flight (a full eight hours longer than my flight to Germany had been), but reclined in a sleeper seat, I slept nine of those hours, woke up to a full English breakfast, watched a movie, and then we were there. Easy peasy.

Everything I knew about the Land Down Under I'd read in books. The books did not prepare me for what awaited. First, Australians were clearly "my people." At once friendly and nice, they loved to get crazy and wild, too, and again, my "stepped up" drag outfits looked tame by comparison. Our hotel room, the presidential suite of the Park Hyatt, overlooked the harbor and Sydney Opera House, and we sat outside on our deck in the mornings just to take in the people, and the sun on the water. Australia's food is as rich and flavorful as its population (for some reason, I remember the tomato juice being particularly yummy and salty), and we consumed as many cosmopolitans (a vodka-based martini drink, mixed with black currant juice instead of cranberry juice in Oz) as we could get our hands on.

The main event, the Mardi Gras parade, was scheduled for March 4, 1995. It would culminate in a giant all-night party at Royal Hall. To prepare, Jeffrey and I went shopping. We picked out short-shorts and tank tops, and Jeffrey also acquired a healthy supply of party drugs, including ecstasy and speed. Cocaine was hard to come by in Oz, so people took speed instead, which wasn't as strong but lasted longer. He still thought the problem was my friends, not my use of drugs.

The parade itself was incredible. Brightly-colored floats, featuring elaborate set pieces and entertainers wearing over-the-top costumes, made their way through downtown and along Centennial Park. Drag queens with cartoonish foam wigs danced with hot boys in leather underwear, many of whom were lean like me, or sculpted and voluptuous—not just the Muscle Marys of LA. I found the whole thing very empowering, very body-positive across the spectrum, and basically just felt like I fit in seamlessly. It was a breath of fresh air for this newly-out gay man.

We followed the performers into Royal Hall, already overflowing with glitter, sequins, feathers, and body paint. Each room within the main hall played a different type of music and attracted a slightly different crowd. Jeffrey and I went from room to room, checking them all out, and circled back by the main stage every couple of hours to watch the next act. Boy George headlined Sydney's Mardi Gras that year.

In one of the side rooms, we ran into Anastasia, the Australian woman who'd been Brett's boyfriend's beard in Salt Lake. Happily, she invited us to join her friends, a motley crew from Melbourne who loved to dance. Right away, I felt drawn to one of her friends: a drag queen named Paris. Her makeup was theatrical and flawless. Her costume was impeccably designed, with fine detail. Naturally quiet, she nevertheless commanded the whole room's attention, like she was the pied piper, and we, the children entranced by her music. It didn't matter that I was high, drunk, and between the flashing lights and pressing bodies, experiencing sensory overload; I wanted to get to know the man behind the makeup better.

Anastasia, her friends, and Jeffrey and I spent the rest of the night together, rotating between the drag queen tent, the leather daddies tent, the techno tent, and the main dance hall. As the sun came up, we followed the crowds to "recovery parties" in the alleys behind several local gay bars (or "hotels," in Aussie parlance). Only once the sunlight had burned away the last of the evening's magic, did we return to our hotel, where we promptly passed out for at least twelve hours. It did me little good. When I woke up, my jaw hurt from the X and the speed,[36] I didn't want to eat, and I'd refuse to leave the room for another twenty-four hours.

Eventually, I recovered, just in time for the Melbourne crew to invite us back to their fair city. Jeffrey thought it sounded fun, so we went south for a few days and got to know our new friends a little better. If I'd liked Sydney, I *loved* Melbourne, where Paris, as the top name in Melbourne's drag scene, got us VIP treatment at any show we wanted to attend. The club owners, and even the random patrons I met at these shows, treated me like royalty—like I was perfectly amazing and interesting. They asked me all kinds of questions about myself and my life, but without expectation, as though there was nothing I needed to be for them beyond who I already was. Between the open and accepting culture, and the upbeat people, who were so easy to love, Australia, I decided, felt more like home than America ever had, or ever would!

Paris's boyfriend, Johnny, asked Jeffrey and I to stay at their flat. Jeffrey refused to stay in anyone's spare room—it just wasn't something he *did*—so we stayed at a four-star hotel nearby. We nevertheless spent almost all of our time together, sharing stories and laughing until our sides hurt over port wine from a box with those two men. A lifelong friendship blossomed there, such that when Jeffrey and I got married, it was Paris who'd stand beside me as my maid of honor.

---

[36] For whatever reason, ecstasy makes you tighten your jaw and chew compulsively. It also, I now believe, has long-term effects on the brain, including permanently disrupting the neurotransmitter serotonin. What I'm experiencing now—heightened anxiety, depression, confusion, and short-term memory problems—I think is the result of using X so heavily.

Me as Vivian in Melbourne, Australia, living
out my Pretty Woman fantasy.

Randos

I said that trip was an "around-the-world" trip, and indeed, from
Australia we traveled to Bangkok, Thailand, and then on to
London, England, where Jeffrey has a flat in Edgerton Gardens.
Bangkok and London, I'm sad to say, passed in a party-hearty
blur of clubs and bars, and before I knew it, we were back to
Utah, and back to our normal routines. To Jeffrey's chagrin, I
picked up precisely where I'd left off (partying with my friends in
Salt Lake City), with one exception: we hired a personal trainer,
Evelyn, and worked out together three times a week. Other than
that, though, while Jeffrey had hoped some time away would do
me good, I hadn't really changed, and neither had he.

The more Jeffrey rode me about my choice of friends and
activities, the more I came to resent his Jim-like approach to
"controlling" me. He didn't want all these "randos" in "his"
house at all hours of the day and night, prompting me to
threaten to get my own place. When Jeffrey protested, I said,
"Maybe we need some time apart to reevaluate our relationship."
I found a condo near the University of Utah, which was closer
to downtown and where I was spending all my time anyway.

Jeffrey loaned me the money to buy the condo, so I could put it in my name, eventually paying me an "employee bonus" large enough to cover the mortgage in full. Having my own place definitely made me feel better and more independent, but Jeffrey hated my new tendency to retreat from him there. He decided we should remodel the condo together, so he had an excuse to stop by more often.

We dreamed big, and taking impromptu dance breaks to Ace of Base's cover of "Don't Turn Around," planned to replace everything from the outdated lacquered cabinets and glass block wall, to the teal, '80s-era carpet. Not long after the remodel started, however, Jeffrey and I had a spectacular fight, and officially broke up for the first of several times. "Finish off the condo," Jeffrey told our interior decorator, "but do it as quickly and inexpensively as possible. I just want out of this thing." Where there was to be travertine and granite, cheap tile and fixtures were installed in their place. I didn't care; the condo was mine, and that's all that mattered.

Infatuated with my newfound autonomy, next I decided to buy another car, one that could also be "all mine," never mind that I'd still be purchasing it with money I'd saved on Jeffrey's payroll. On my next trip home to McAllen (Mom and I had since patched up our relationship the best we could), I answered a newspaper ad for a Nissan 300ZX, a slightly sportier car than the Mitsubishi 3000 GT. It had been listed for sale by one Enrique Cruz, a dealer then working from his home. When I showed up at his house, I think both of us could tell the other was gay, and we felt like kindred spirits. Homophobia was still rampant in the Valley, especially in the Latino community, but around each other, Enrique and I could be ourselves.

"You know," Enrique said, after we'd been chatting for a while, "you should consider getting your dealer's license in Texas. Then you could save paying sales tax and registration on any car you might buy in the future."

The idea appealed to me. I missed fixing up and selling cars like I had in Germany. Before I could really think about doing that, though, I had more serious matters in Texas to tend.

A Bunch of Beeping, Blinking Machines

Around the time I'd separated from the Air Force, in July 1994, my father, Phillip Flamer, had been diagnosed with colon cancer. Initially, his prognosis was good. His doctors expected him to respond well to the chemotherapy, and we all adopted a fairly relaxed "wait and see" policy. By Spring 1995, however, when Jeffrey and I were smack in the middle of renovating my condo, Dad's cancer, we found out, had metastasized to his stomach. "It's terminal," they said. "You may want to prepare yourselves."

Although Mom and I were still sorting out our differences, it was important to me to spend as much time as possible in Texas during these months, even if it meant occasionally crossing paths with her. For the most part, Dad and his wife Ava were still in McAllen, except for when he had to go to MD Anderson in Houston for treatment. Then I would stay in a hotel next to the hospital; otherwise, I stayed with Dad and Ava, or Gramaw and Grampa Green, depending on who was available.

After I bought the Nissan 300ZX from Enrique, I left it in McAllen for a while, so I had reliable transportation whenever I landed at McAllen International Airport. In early April 1995, things took a definitive turn for the worse; at that point, I pretty much moved to Houston full-time for the next two months, until he passed June 9, 1995.

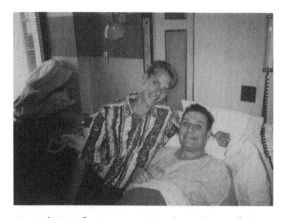

Spending a few precious weeks with my father,
Phillip Flamer, before he passed.

Toward the end, a bunch of blinking, beeping machines
were all that was keeping my father alive. It's my opinion that
once he'd had the initial surgery to remove his colon cancer,
resulting in a permanent colostomy bag, he was so saddened
over his quality of life that he gave up the fight. To be sure, his
decline was quick and physically graphic. I wasn't there when
he breathed his last breath. I'd flown home to see Jeffrey because
I needed a break, and three or four days later Dad pulled the
ventilator out of his own accord, and that was it. Ava's sister
was the only one present, which I believe made it easier for my
dad to let go. When we got the news, Jeffrey chartered a private
jet for us to fly back. He never got off the plane, though, as he
knew my family wouldn't have wanted him there.

My dad was fifty-two when he died—an age that, at time
of writing, is just around the corner for me. He left nothing,
not a single asset, behind him when he went. I think about
my childhood with him, compared to the months we spent
together in 1995, and find peace in the fact that we were never
closer than we were at the end. Still, I chose not to come out
to my father, for two reasons: 1) It hadn't exactly gone over

well with Mom; and 2) Regardless of what his reaction might have been, it nevertheless would have added undue stress to his situation, something my stepmother pointed out repeatedly. She claimed Dad wouldn't have accepted me—that my coming out would have made everything harder, and tainted our final days together. In reality, these were *her* thoughts and opinions. I like to believe he would have been okay with it; if not at first, then eventually. I'll never know for sure, though—only that I loved him, and continue to miss him.

Three months after Dad died, his mother, Grandma Gussie, suffered a stroke and also died. There's no doubt in my mind that my father's death caused hers. At 89, she'd been alone for several years, after Grandpa Morris had succumbed to any one of the serious medical problems—prostate cancer, diabetes, you name it—that he was dealing with. Still, she flew on a plane by herself to attend my father's funeral. I remember all three of them warmly, and it is with pride that I carry the Flamer name today.

Lines in the Sand

After my father's funeral, I drove the 300ZX back to Utah, stopping in Dallas along the way to visit my cousin Isabella. I stayed for a weekend and was relieved to party the time, and the dark pall of death, away. The drug dealer I found in the first club she took me to sold me ecstasy laced with heroin— another first. It was predictably amazing, and instantly hooked, I bought a hundred more tablets to bring back with me to Salt Lake. He then offered me something I'd never heard of: GHB. Short for gamma hydroxybutyrate, GHB is in the same class of drugs as ketamine and rohypnol—a.k.a., the "date-rape" drugs. When properly dosed, however, GHB won't induce a coma, but will increase the user's sense of wellbeing and confidence, while reducing inhibitions and sometimes acting like an aphrodisiac.

"It's like X, but without the come-down," this dealer said. In other words, GHB doesn't deplete your dopamine, which is what makes you stare into the existential abyss after a hard night of ecstasy. "You just don't want to mix it with alcohol."

I was scared to try it. Ever the hypochondriac, I wanted to do some more research on GHB first before subjecting my body to it. Isabella talked me into it, though, pointing out that the drug was commonly used by doctors as an anesthetic, and was therefore a "less dangerous, more natural" alternative to ecstasy. So, I did it, and I loved it, and I'd soon add this chemical into my regularly rotating repertoire.

Back in Utah, I finished off my condo and enjoyed distributing my heroin-laced X haul to friends. The people I'd met before we left for Australia—Eric, Bryce, Elizabeth, and Carla—started coming around more often, Carla especially. She stayed over so frequently that she soon moved into the second bedroom, at which point Jeffrey attempted to "buy her off" like he had with Dylan. Carla didn't take the bait, though. "I value Paul's friendship more than your money," she told Jeffrey, proving that he'd been wrong about my friends: they really did like me for me, and not simply for what I could give them.[37] It probably baffled Jeffrey not to get his way, and to feel

---

[37] Yes and no. Carla was a complicated case. Although we'd met in a gay bar and she knew, point-blank, that I was gay and with Jeffrey, she managed to develop feelings for me anyway. She told me she was in love with me, and that she wanted to have sex with me, which is how I ended up sleeping with a woman for the third time. It was a mistake: I came home high and horny, and there she was. I didn't know she was a virgin, or I *definitely* wouldn't have slept with her. The next day, on top of that guilt, I spent coming down from an

excluded from the circle he thought he'd always be a part of. He and I were still mostly on the outs, anyway, so it's not like he had a significant other's "right" to control who I saw and when.

Unable to "get through" to me, Jeffrey took to writing more letters: long, thoughtful missives that alternately condemned my choices and pleaded with me to come back to him. They said things like, "Your goals seem to have gone out the window, Paul. You seem to have no willpower at all." Or: "What am I supposed to do? The way things are, you only give me two choices. I can … get drug-fucked every weekend with you and your new 'friends,' or I can go to bed alone and wonder where you are and what you are doing. That is not much of a choice, is it?"

He was right, of course. Like the Paul who once thought setting his car on fire was a good idea, I was back to making stupid decisions, and kicking to the curb what few good things I still had going for me. But I was mad. Mad about my dad dying. Mad about my family's rejection of me. Mad that my life had no discernible point, and that nothing I did made me feel any happier. I hated myself, and because you can't love other people unless you love yourself, I turned to the one person on the planet who was telling me, in no uncertain terms, that he loved me, and I gave him a heartfelt "Fuck you."

One afternoon, completely beside himself with hurt and helplessness, Jeffrey stormed into my condo. He yelled at me like he had never yelled before, and it triggered me to again conflate Jeffrey with my stepfather Jim. Having walked out on Jim, I picked up my keys to walk out on Jeffrey, but when he saw I

---

ecstasy binge. Terrible. Afterward, Carla wanted to go everywhere together, do everything together, and because I'm a pleaser, I couldn't push her away. Jeffrey telling me I couldn't have Carla in my life only reinforced my attachment to her, even though it really served neither one of us.

intended to leave, he threw me onto the couch and held me down. The only "weapon" within reaching distance was a pair of my heavy combat boots from the Air Force. I picked them up and slammed them on to the glass top of the nearby coffee table, shattering it into a million pieces. Instinctively, Jeffrey curled into a ball, shielding his head against the flying glass, and I seized my opportunity to run out to the garage. I jumped into my Porsche[38] and sped off, failing to remember until I was clear of the parking garage that Carla was still in the condo.

Apparently, Jeffrey had figured this out. He was banging on her bedroom door, trying to break it down, when the police arrived. She'd called 911 when she'd heard the table break. The cops called me next on my cell phone. "Can you come back?" they asked. "We'll make Jeffrey leave, but we need to get a statement from you."

As I was walking back into the building, Jeffrey was walking out. "I'm sorry," he said. I could tell he meant it.

"Call me when you're ready to talk peacefully," I said.

Prior to this day, Jeffrey had never displayed a temper. He was controlling, yes, but in the way of people who are used

---

[38] Jeffrey had given me a white Porsche 911 convertible for Christmas 1994. I had this car in addition to a new '95 Mitsubishi 3000 GT, which I'd purchased to replace the '93, and a yellow '92 Mazda Miata that I'd bought while living at the Bountiful apartment. After only a few months of owning it, I'd also recently traded the 300ZX in for an SUV, so I could ferry my friends around town. Ford had just come out with the second-generation Explorer in late 1994/early 1995; I bought the wild purple floor model that the manager insisted was "just for show" after calling in a favor from a friend at another dealership. The following year, Jeffrey would buy us matching black Range Rovers, at which point I gave the Explorer to his friend Ruth. All told, I probably owned twenty or thirty different cars while I was with Jeffrey—no less than five cars at a time.

to having money, and thereby, power. People respected Jeffrey; but that day, I feared him, and as it had a decade before in Houston with Jim, the fear fueled my anger. Only now, I was an adult, with a grown man's sense of agency.

"No matter how upset I make you," I told Jeffrey the next time we talked, "you are never to put your hands on me. Ever." Jeffrey swore he would respect that boundary, and for the rest of our relationship, he did.

I'm not always great at drawing lines in the sand, as for most of my life, I was too afraid that people wouldn't come with me. Better to play by their rules, I thought, if it meant keeping them in my life. After I came out to my mom, brother, and sister, though, I realized that as painful as speaking my truth—and in the process, losing them[39]—had been, not living my truth had been worse. I'd invited them in, and they'd rudely declined, but it hadn't canceled the whole party. My life was still mine to live, whether I made good choices or bad from there on out, and this realization gave me my power. I started standing up for myself, and what and who I wanted in my life, and setting firm boundaries accordingly.

It's scary, when what you know to be right clashes with the people you want to keep around. Luckily, Jeffrey recognized the mistake he'd made, and his bigness helped to inspire mine. I didn't quit drugs or stop pissing my youth and health away right that minute, but I would once the boundaries I was forced to set were for myself.

---

[39] The loss of Peter and Joy, at least, was not permanent. They were 21 and 18, respectively, when I came out, and while that should have been old enough to think for themselves, they let Mom's poison cloud their judgment for a few more years yet. Joy was still living at home and very much under Mom's influence. Pete was in the military, and drinking that Kool-Aid. Eventually, though, they came around, and our relationships healed more swiftly and with less scarring than mine and my mother's did.

10

Supermodel of the World Lands in California

RuPaul, my drag queen idol, has a television show called *RuPaul's Drag Race*, in which queens compete for the title of America's Next Drag Superstar and a cash prize. Each new season opens with thirteen contestants, who are whittled down until only three remain. They then go head to head. That's one kind of "drag race."

In car terms, a drag race is when two drivers, behind the wheels of two different vehicles, compete side-by-side in an acceleration contest. They race in a straight line from a standing start, and the first to cross the finish line wins the race. Jeffrey's and my relationship was like a drag race, each of us competing against the other for dominance, and what remained of our affections.

The competition took many, sometimes subtle, forms. For my twenty-fifth birthday, for example, Jeffrey hosted a total blowout—half birthday party, half apology for the scene he'd made at the condo. It was a way for him to prove his love for me, to demonstrate how he put me first. In return, though, I'd be expected to do the same: to "prove" my love for him by leaving my friends in the dust. I didn't understand that at first, so when Jeffrey asked how he could make my birthday "extra special" that year, I thought about it for a moment, then joked, "I'd like RuPaul to sing me Happy Birthday."

"Okay," Jeffrey said, the picture of seriousness. "I'll see what I can do."

He was joking, too—right?

As it turned out, Jeffrey knew the owner of Bricks (the bar at which we'd met). He booked the whole venue, then contacted RuPaul's management in LA, and hired him for the night of August 17, 1995. I couldn't believe it. All Jeffrey had to do was snap his fingers and things happened!

I wore a Versace checkered vest to my party. Whitney Houston, TLC, and Cher drowned out the easy conversation of two hundred invited guests. Onstage, RuPaul gave the performance of a lifetime, and then he asked me, the birthday boy, to join him. High as a kite, I barely recall singing "Supermodel" alongside the queen herself, though video clips from this night reveal that when she sang "Turn to the left," I turned to the right, and vice versa.[40] How mortifying! I didn't care, though. It was one of the best nights—and by far, one of the best birthdays—of my life.

---

[40]   Another symptom of undiagnosed dyslexia, like the way I get numbers backward when I try to type a phone number, or can't discern the number of ones and zeroes in a large sum? Who knows.

For my twenty-fifth birthday, we invited RuPaul to perform in Salt Lake City. We sold tickets to the event for $5 and in that way raised money for his charity. He brought me onstage to sing a song with him, but I was so excited (and so high) that I couldn't remember the words. It was probably the best birthday I've ever had, as I've always looked up to RuPaul. He even autographed one of the lanyards we had made for the event, just for me (along with a t-shirt and five pairs of high-heeled shoes).

But then it came time for Jeffrey to call up his favor, the concession I was obliged to offer him. "I want to buy us a new house, Paul," Jeffrey said. "One in downtown Salt Lake City, so you can be closer to the clubs. I'll even put it in your name, okay? Only…"—and here was the clincher—"…you have to sell the condo and live with me there. And none of your friends can 'move in,' even temporarily. Also, we would have to agree on who can visit, and for how long."

Reading what I just typed right now, I don't know why I ever thought that was a fair deal. I already had my own place, where I could be independent and entertain whenever and whomever I wished. But I think I knew if I said no now, I would in effect be saying goodbye to Jeffrey, who had hit the upper limits of his tolerance. I wasn't ready to let him go, so I said yes.[41] We then verbally affirmed our renewed commitment to each other and the relationship.

In September, we found our new home: a two-bed, four-bath single-family home near the state capitol. Built in the 1980s, it was all orange wood and brass plating—a decorator's nightmare and the total opposite of my style. Jeffrey suggested I spearhead the remodel this time, picking out everything from the colors to the furnishings. I chose green marble for the bathrooms, with bright, clean chrome throughout, and ordered all the wood be lightened or whitewashed. The one piece Jeffrey contributed, as a gift to me, was a custom fountain for the entryway. It was made of brushed aluminum and styled like two intersecting slides, which symbolized, he said, the two of us. I loved it, and I loved that house, once it looked exactly the way I wanted it to, top to bottom.

---

[41] My only regret was that in agreeing to sell the condo, I was displacing Carla, too. But then, that had been Jeffrey's plan all along. She found someone else to stay with short-term, we saw each other less and less, and then she finally moved back to California. That was good for Carla. She finished college, which all the partying in Salt Lake City had prevented her from doing, and met a man who would ultimately take her to Las Vegas, where we would meet again.

While renovations were underway, we leased a penthouse in the American Towers. The penthouse belonged to Valerie Jones, Jeffrey's friend and a real estate agent whose husband was twenty years younger than she (something else the two of them had in common). Everything in the penthouse was peach-colored, down to the wood parquet floors. Thus, we called it the Peach Palace.

Working out in heels and a wig with Evelyn, our personal trainer, at the "Peach Palace" penthouse while our State Capitol home was being remodeled. Evelyn and I would become close and I would use our hour workout as a therapy session.

Sleaze Ball

All told, the State Capitol home remodel took six months—long enough for us to begin to go stir-crazy in the cramped, beautiful penthouse. We took frequent trips just to get out and shake things up, first to Sleaze Ball in Fall '95, and then to Mardi Gras again in the spring. Like Mardi Gras Sydney, Sleaze Ball was an LGBT-oriented fetish festival celebrated annually in Australia. *More 'sleazy' than Mardi Gras?* I remember thinking when Jeffrey suggested it. *I'm all in!*

The theme that year was "A Robodyke and Cyberfag Homosphere," held on September 30, 1995. We had a great time checking out the event and catching up with all our new "old" friends from Melbourne.

I had lately begun studying up on GHB like I once had with ecstasy, learning most of what I knew about sourcing and dosing the drug from a book called *Better Sex through Chemistry*. Not only was GHB still legal at the time, it was commonly sold in health food stores as a supplement for bodybuilders. At Sleaze Ball, I turned all my Aussie friends onto the drug. So long as we didn't mix it with alcohol, GHB helped us maintain a happy, fog-like distance from the reality of a world that didn't like or accept who we were. Like the Dallas dealer said, it was basically ecstasy with a slightly lower peak, minus the existential crash! The ten or so of us went through the one bottle I'd brought with me so fast that I had a friend in LA overnight another bottle to us.

In late February 1996, we returned for Mardi Gras Sydney. Tony, who by this time had quit working for Delta, earned his real estate license, and was working for Jeffrey's foundation and as Jeffrey's private real estate agent, came with us.[42] So did Ron, Jeffrey's friend and the owner of Brick's nightclub. We had another typically amazing time, stopping in Singapore on the

---

[42] Tony came with us, but his boyfriend (not Hal; they'd since broken up) did not. While we were gone in Australia, this boyfriend "broke into" (he'd somehow acquired a spare key fob) the Peach Palace, "borrowed" the keys to my beloved Porsche 911, and took it for a joy ride—or several. He then scraped it all to shit trying to sneak back into the American Towers parking garage. I never noticed the damage because he took the car to a body shop, had it repaired, and replaced the vehicle all before we came home. I don't remember how I discovered this, only that it ended my friendship with Tony.

way back, as well as London (on the way back from Sleaze Ball, we'd stopped in Hong Kong instead of Bangkok or Singapore, but London was always on the itinerary).

Life wasn't just one big party, though. Jeffrey and I used these trips like distractions from our increasingly turbulent home life. When we weren't partying, we were fighting about my growing dependence on drugs, and the future of a relationship that had never really been healthy, born as it was amidst ex-boyfriends, alcohol, and other secrets. While the State Capitol home remodel continued in the background, our romantic life reached a breaking point there in the suffocating Peach Palace. I threatened to move out and move on from Jeffrey. I even knew where I would go: my friends Lance and Pat had a spare bedroom in their Avenues home, not far from downtown. But then Jeffrey lured me back with the promise of *another* new house—this one in Beverly Hills, the place that had inspired my drag name, Vivian. I'd wanted to live there ever since visiting two years before. Against my better judgment, I flew to LA with Jeffrey, and fell in love with another fixer-upper house on Rodeo Drive in the 90210 zip code. "Would you live here with me if I bought it for you for Valentine's Day?" Jeffrey asked.

"Yes!" I breathed, wondering if I hadn't accidentally laced my morning coffee with GHB. Surely I was hallucinating this moment.

Alas, it was Jeffrey I was addicted to, and the wild mood swings of our up-and-down relationship. When things were good, they were *so* good; when things were bad—as was more often the case—they were terrible. But then would come another new vacation, car, house—another bribe, always—and we would temporarily reconcile.

Until the next time.

Three. Two. One.

During a rare period of peace, Jeffrey turned forty-eight. I wanted to repay the favor of bringing RuPaul in for my birthday, and asked Jeffrey who he would like to have perform. "Chaka Khan," Jeffrey said—the Queen of Funk. Ron and I secured her for Jeffrey's party, and it was spectacular. For once, he, not I, was the center of attention: a good thing for Jeffrey, and a better one for our relationship.

The next night, I invited a few drag friends who were then staying in the American Towers condo just below the Peach Palace to join me for an evening of relaxation and meth. We were already high when Jeffrey picked another fight— our biggest yet, and the crack in the iceberg before the sheet broke off completely—about the same tired issue of control. Jeffrey had too much of it, most egregiously over me. I didn't have enough control, most notably over myself. "You're right, Jeffrey," I agreed, nodding my head manically and gesturing at the world around me, my shocked-into-silence friends included. "My life *is* out of control. I know that all I do is party, party, party. But have you ever stopped to wonder why?"

"What do you mean?"

"I mean, I don't even own my identity anymore, Jeffrey. All I am to anyone is 'Jeffrey's boyfriend.' I have no job, nothing that I've worked toward or own that *you* haven't given to me. 'Paul,' the person, literally doesn't exist. I have no doubt that, on some unconscious level, I'm just trying to make reality fit the facts."

"How can I help you, Paul? I want to help."

"Forget it," I said wearily. "I'm done fighting with you. I'm moving out." Leaving Joey and Raven in the living room, I walked into the bedroom to pack my bags. Jeffrey ran in after me. Angry at being embarrassed in front of my friends, he grabbed my checkbook and AMEX card, and yelled, "Fine, go if you want. But you're not taking these with you."

"Give them back!" I demanded. Jeffrey responded by running into the bathroom and locking the door. "Open this door or I'll kick it down!" I screamed.

When he didn't answer: "You have to the count of three. Three. Two. One." *Here goes.*

I kicked the door until it started cracking. Inside, I heard Jeffrey retreat into the water closet and lock that door, too. Once I got through the first door, I again counted to three, fully intending to kick the water closet door in as well. On "two," Jeffrey opened the door, threw both the card and the checkbook at me, and relocked the door.

We didn't speak for the rest of the night.

While it felt as though I'd "won" the argument, the truth was, I didn't have a good answer for Jeffrey. I didn't know how to help myself, never mind how to let Jeffrey help me. So he came up with his own proposal. In a letter dated April 1996, Jeffrey wrote: "I have learned that the biggest step to gaining self-worth comes when we stop being obsessed with what others think of us. Our worth is within." He then suggested, to help me rediscover my self-worth, he would loan me two million dollars. "You could invest it," he said. "Earn your own income—money that's honestly *yours*. You can pay me back whenever you want, and keep the rest."

He drew up the promissory note and introduced me to someone he knew at Goldman Sachs. Just before the transfer went through, though, Jeffrey changed his mind. He decided he'd rather "gift" me two hundred thousand dollars, no strings attached, to invest however I wanted. I accepted the gift and invested it immediately, lest I spend it unwisely, but nothing else about my lifestyle changed.

That summer, we moved into the State Capitol home. I had people over against Jeffrey's wishes. We fought. In a moment of passion, we broke up.

Suddenly calmer and more in control than I'd felt in months, I grabbed the bag I'd started packing the night of the water closet fight and walked out. I moved in with Lance and Pat, where I stayed (when I wasn't traveling) for the next two months.

Hey, Girl!

Lance and Pat were entrepreneurs and house-flippers, forever on the hunt for the next opportunity. After I'd lived with them for about a month, they told me they were planning to move to Orange County, California—a "fresh start," they said, after Salt Lake's incestuous, backbiting, and drug-ridden gay scene. "Want to come with us, Paul?" they asked. "We'll help you find a house to flip, and split the profit. Deal?" Lance and Pat were also into cars, and since I'd recently taken Enrique Cruz's advice and gotten my Texas dealer's license, I thought buying and selling cars as well as houses in California sounded like just the ticket for me.

Believe it or not, no one was happier about this development than my mother. She and I were tentatively writing letters to one another again, and when I told her that Jeffrey and I had broken up, and I was thinking about moving to California, she offered to come out to Utah to help me move. Salt Lake City was a "den of sin" as far as she was concerned; she would do anything to get me out of there! Plus, although she'd never admit it, I think Mom was a tiny bit curious. Who was this mysterious billionaire boyfriend? What was my life in Ski City, USA actually like?

Mom and I spent a few days packing up my belongings in a yellow Ryder moving truck. To thank her for her time and assistance, I took her out each night for a new experience, inviting all of my straight friends to join us. We went to a sports game.

We went out to eat. Madison Taylor, my friend and a TV actress, generously hosted us for dinner at her house one evening. Mom even met Lance and Pat, the gay couple I'd been living with, and didn't bat an eye at their relationship. It helped that both of them were "masc for masc," short for "masculine for masculine." In other words, they acted very neutral, very "straight" if you will. They didn't wear lip liner and mascara like some guys I knew did, so Mom felt more comfortable around them.

That changed when we got to Newport Beach. I'd put an offer on, and subsequently bought,[43] a bank-owned house that turned out to be an excellent investment. Twenty-eight hundred square feet, it had three bedrooms and two-and-a-half bathrooms. We unloaded the barest necessities—mattresses to sleep on; toiletries to shower with—and conked out, only to be greeted first thing in the morning by my mother's worst nightmare. Chris Brown, one of Lance's friends whom no one could tell was gay just by looking at him (until he opened his mouth, that is), sauntered in with a loud and sassy "Hey, girl!" He proceeded to hug and kiss us three men on both cheeks, which was happening as Mom walked in from the garage. Shocked, she nearly dropped the stack of dishes she was carrying! With a look of horror on her face, she grabbed the first set of car keys she saw and ran out the front door. She drove to a nearby hotel, checked herself in, and told me to change her plane ticket home to the next day. It would be the last time she ever visited me at that home, or any of my homes in California. She'd made a good effort at stepping out of her comfort zone, but there'd be no repeat performance.

---

[43] It helped that Jeffrey had offered to be the lien holder for the house, meaning I'd be paying him back as though he were the bank. Even though we were broken up, it was a way for him to stay relevant in my life, and I think he always hoped we'd get back together.

Chris Brown, the friend who scandalized my mother.

Back in Utah, Jeffrey was biding his time, waiting for me to "come to my senses" and move home to him. He sent me more letters during the summer and fall of 1996 than ever before: sincere proclamations of love and regret, and confrontational examinations alike. One letter from July 1996 reads:

> I have never loved anyone like I have loved you, so I guess it makes sense that I have never hurt like I hurt right now. ... [but] I will survive. I will find someone who wants to be with me. Most of all, I hope you will learn to love yourself. You have a lot more to offer someone than just sex. I wish you could believe that. Remember that I loved you totally without shame and without any regret.

The next month, in August, he wrote: "Who will be there for you when you are alone? When you are afraid? When you are in trouble? When you are sick? I know you don't want me there, but you need someone."

I have *someone*, I thought when I read that. *Two someones, actually—Lance and Pat.* I didn't know then that, true to form, Jeffrey was working on expunging them from my life, too.

Lance and Pat hadn't sold their house in Utah before we'd all moved to California, so one weekend they went back to get the house ready for sale. Hearing they were in town, Jeffrey stopped by and offered to take them to dinner. "I still really love Paul," he told my two friends over steaks at the New Yorker restaurant. "Do you think you could convince him to give us one last chance?"

"I don't know," Lance said, uneasy. "Paul's trying to work on himself in Newport Beach. The change of environment has been good for him. Maybe you need to let him go."

"I can't," Jeffrey persisted. "Please talk to him for me. He'll listen if it comes from you. If it helps," he added, "you can have my Mercedes."

He meant his Mercedes S600 sedan—the car he'd driven them to dinner in. The car he knew for a fact Lance loved. That was Jeffrey: still using money and gifts to bribe people into doing his bidding.

While Lance and Pat were gone, I entertained myself by adopting a dog, a miniature schnauzer that I named Lucas, and dancing with him around the living room to Mariah Carey's "Always Be My Baby." Lance already had a dog named Chloe. I wanted something to take care of, and to love me; it seemed like the thing to do. When they got back, two doggos ran to greet them at the door. If Lance and Pat were surprised or concerned about my ability to care for a pet, they didn't say anything. What they did tell me about was their run-in with Jeffrey, minus the whole Mercedes business (they never planned to take him up on it, they said). After much careful thought and consideration, I decided I still loved Jeffrey, too. I wanted to work things out with him. Had our three months, and as many states, apart been enough?

Jeffrey was elated by my decision. "Let's all go to Sleaze Ball to celebrate!" he said. "Everyone—you, me, Lance, and Pat!" As the festival was scheduled for the first week of October, it was perfect timing to get the four of us together. Jeffrey flew out to California the week before, so we could all fly to Sydney together from LA. That week, he took me to see a new piece of property in Laguna Beach. It was closer to my house in Orange County than the Beverly Hills house (which was still being renovated), the idea being that we might share it, now that we were boyfriends again. The house, of course, was beyond gorgeous. In addition to a private stretch of beach, and a bedroom whose ceiling literally opened up like a sunroof above the 360-degree rotating bed (clad in Versace sheets), it had an eight-car garage, inside of which was parked a Porsche 928— just like the one Sergeant Wally had let me drive when I was stationed in Germany.

All for a cool $17.5 million.

"What do you think?" Jeffrey wanted to know.

"Only if they'll throw in the car," I joked.

Unbeknownst to me, Jeffrey passed my silly request onto the real estate agent, who confirmed with the elderly couple selling the house: Yes, they'd include the Porsche in the sale. My jaw hit the floor. Had Jeffrey seriously just dropped seventeen mil without blinking? The house went into escrow as we boarded our plane to Down Under.

Wedding of the Century

The Sleaze Ball theme in October 1996 was "Voodoo Circus," probably the most fitting name possible for the months that followed. Everything that happened between October and January was a complete and utter circus, including my marriage to one billionaire named Jeffrey.

He proposed in his London flat, after we'd left the chaos of Australia and recovered somewhat on Thailand's dreamy beaches. "Yes!" I accepted, as happy as I was exhausted by the recent rollercoaster ride of our relationship. Like many before me, I made the mistake of thinking a formalized commitment would somehow erase our obvious problems.

"Wouldn't it be fun to be in drag for the ceremony?" I asked, halfway kidding.

"It's fine with me if that's what you want," Jeffrey said. It's what he always said to get me to go along with him—"Whatever you want, Paul."

Walking one day among the cheerful shops of London's New Bond Street, where Princess Di was wont to shop, we wandered into David Morris, a high-end boutique selling bespoke and bridal jewelry. There, Jeffrey and I ordered custom green diamond wedding rings to the tune of 90,000 pounds (or $120,000) apiece. He then took me shopping for my wedding dress. I saw the perfect one—a silver Isabella Christiansen—from half a block away: It was draped on a mannequin in the window. We went inside. "Is that gown for sale?" I asked "Let me try it on."

My wedding ring: a one-and-a-half carat yellow-green diamond.
It retailed for 95,000 pounds—about $110,000 USD.

The salesperson carefully took it off the mannequin. It had a $30,000 price tag, but it fit me perfectly (off the rack, with no alterations other than sewing padding into the chest, despite being cut for a runway model) and I was worth it. Another *Pretty Woman* moment for Vivian.

"Great," I said, as the bemused clerk wrapped up the dress for me. "I'll take that black one, too," pointing to a beaded gown with matching black Jimmy Choo shoes.

"Anything you want, Paul," my special, wonderful fiancé repeated.

We arrived back to California in early November, giving us almost no time at all to get the Laguna Beach house ready for a mid-December wedding. We planned to get married in the house's grand entryway, a two-story atrium, with sixty-odd guests from around the world as our witnesses. To make it feasible for everyone to attend on such short notice, Jeffrey bought all of the guests' airfare and also put them up stateside. Paris, my drag queen friend from Melbourne, agreed to be my maid of honor and do my makeup for the big day. Jeffrey's brother served as his best man, and the brother's wife, Lisa, became my other bridesmaid. Evelyn, my personal trainer, said that without my father there, she'd walk me down the aisle. My gay cousin Greg attended (Greg and his husband, and Jeffrey and his husband are good friends to this day). No one else from my family came. Madison Taylor, my actress friend, brought her daughters, and Bob, a gay ex-Catholic priest, officiated. It all came together at the last minute, but was truly the wedding of the century.[44] When I said "I do" to Jeffrey, I believed I meant forever.[45]

---

[44] It was the wedding of the century in everything but name, as gay marriage wasn't legal yet in 1996.

[45] I'll add here that Jeffrey asked me, before we married, to sign a prenuptial agreement, and I refused. "Why even get married then?" I remember asking him. "Prenups are for people who don't think

Jeffrey and I got married at Pacific Reflections—a seventeen-million-dollar mansion he bought specifically for the wedding. It had a spiral staircase that led down to a glass-floor balcony and out to a private beach on the Pacific coast. On my wedding day, I wore two different gowns with matching feather boas, topped off with a floor-length cape. Paris did my hair and makeup.

---

it'll work out." Jeffrey said, "You're right," and dropped the issue. Later, when he took me to court and tried to claim we'd never had a wedding, I wished I'd signed that document after all, if simply as proof.

Evelyn, my trainer, walked me down the aisle. An ex-priest named
Bob (pictured here) officiated. Later, when I sued Jeffrey, my
"husband" told his lawyer our wedding was "just a big costume
party." Okay. To me, this photo is pretty wedding-esque.

After the ceremony, I swapped my silver gown out for the
black beaded dress, and we partied late into the night. Mariah
Carey's "Fantasy" brought the house down.

We never did take a honeymoon, opting instead to split
up for a week and visit our separate families. While Jeffrey flew
back to Utah to see his kids, I flew home to Texas to spend
Christmas[46] with Mom (yes, she'd forgiven me for the Chris
Brown incident), Pete, Joy, Aunt Jessica, and Grampa and
Gramaw Green. I awoke on Christmas morning on the couch
in my mother's Austin trailer, where she'd been living since
selling her house in McAllen a few years back. In the wake of
the world's most decadent wedding, I felt bad. She told us she'd
sold her house because she was tired of making house payments

---

[46] Even though Jeffrey and I didn't spend our first Christmas as
husband and husband together, he knocked it out of the park with
his gift to me: a yellow Ferrari F355 Spider. I'd seen that exact car
in a Beverly Hills showroom, and Jeffrey remembered how much I
had coveted it. The Ferrari joined the rest of my growing personal
collection, now split between Laguna Beach and Newport Beach.

and wanted to own her residence outright, but here she was sleeping in a trailer while I lived in a palace. Before anyone else came over for lunch, I asked her if I could buy her a house. "Not because I'm better than you," I clarified, "but because you deserve it. No one has to know it came from me."

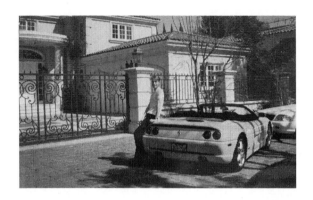

My beautiful yellow Ferrari: Jeffrey's Christmas present to me the year we married, taken in front of the Beverly Hills house on Rodeo Drive.

She declined,[47] saying she was comfortable where she was, though I understood the unspoken: While Jeffrey and I had 'legitimized' our relationship, I was still, in her eyes, a man whore. She didn't want a house that came from her gay son's husband, just like she didn't want a gay son.

I wished she could be happy for me, as *I* was finally happy for me. Jeffrey and I had quit drag racing against each other and at long last joined the same team. What I didn't realize (and maybe Mom did, in the way mothers always seem to know) is

---

[47] A few months later, Mom would take me up on my offer, letting me buy her a duplex in northwest Austin. This will be an important part of the story in chapter eleven.

how I was still competing against myself. And when you race against yourself, you inevitably lose, as at the moment a winner gets declared, so does, by implication, last place.

11

Pedal to the Metal

Jeffrey and I rang in the New Year (1997) in Utah. Our future, as glimpsed through the horse blinders of newly-wedded bliss, seemed bright. Then, on one of their return visits to Salt Lake, Lance and Pat sat me down, and with heavy hearts, confessed: "We didn't tell you the whole story, Paul. About Jeffrey. When he asked us to convince you to go back to him? Well ... he also tried to bribe us with his Mercedes."

What? Had I heard them correctly?

"We wouldn't have said anything about it, except that when the four us then went to Sleaze Ball together, Jeffrey treated us so badly any time you weren't around, talking down to us and saying we should be more grateful to him. We thought you should know."

"Oh my God. I'm so sorry," I said, my mind reeling at 6000 RPM.

I called Jeffrey to verify on the spot. "Is it true?" I demanded, after filling him in on what Lance and Pat had relayed.

He stuttered his way through several excuses, before finally admitting it was true. "I can't believe you went behind my back like that," I accused. "The least you can do is to give them the Mercedes now. We got back together, so you should honor your word."

149

Jeffrey didn't like that. He whined about wanting to keep the car. In the end, he bought Lance and Pat a similar, albeit less expensive, car to square up and calm me down—a "copout deal" eerily reminiscent of the time he'd made me, and then revoked, a two-million-dollar investment offer.

I couldn't stay mad at Jeffrey forever, though, because soon it was February: time for our third annual trip to Mardi Gras Sydney. Just the two of us went, with Paris and Johnny anxiously awaiting us. As usual, we started in Sydney for the parade, followed by the drug-laden all-hours after-party. By the time we'd made it to Melbourne, Jeffrey and I were fighting again. I left him in our Melbourne hotel and went to stay at Paris and Johnny's flat. The writing on the wall, once in cursive script and harder to read, was now clear as day: Our relationship was fractured beyond repair. Having taken my vows[48] just two months earlier, though, I thought, *If anyone's going to end this marriage, it will have to be Jeffrey, not me.*

An Angel

We made it back to the States for the first days of spring, which brought with them a sense of freshness and hope. Something that helped was having five different houses in which to spread out (and find respite from each other): the Orem Manor, the State Capitol home in Salt Lake City, the Beverly Hills mansion (*still* under renovation—we'd yet to live in it at this point), my flip-house in Newport Beach, and the Laguna Beach house where we'd gotten married. At times, we spent a week or more

---

[48] I know our vows meant a lot to Jeffrey, too, as in February 1997, he wrote this in a letter: "On our wedding day, I'm sure I was the happiest man on earth." Both of us hoped our happiness would last longer than it did.

apart, and you know what they say: Absence makes the heart grow fonder. I gifted Lucas, my miniature schnauzer, to Jeffrey on his birthday so Jeffrey could feel like I was always there with him, and he quickly fell in love with the dog. That was a win for everyone, I think—Lucas, most especially.

With more time left to my own devices, I started going out again, usually in LA. I'd hit up the clubs, then drive back to Newport or Laguna late at night, occasionally after drinking or snorting too much. Jeffrey continued to look down on my partying (what little he actually knew about), and in the summer of 1997, it led to a nuclear disaster. Whatever he said that night at the Laguna Beach house made me angry enough to leave. I called up some friends to meet me at the Boom Boom Room, a local Laguna hangout, where we all drank heavily and did ecstasy. At the end of our evening, I drove back to Newport Beach, not Laguna Beach, to avoid Jeffrey.

My friend Terry was in the car with me. He was messing with the Mercedes's rearview mirror while I was driving and managed to break it off the windshield. Instantly enraged, I started driving faster and more erratically. I took the sharp corner into the gated entrance too quickly, causing the car to slide and crash into one of the neighbor's cars parked outside the gate. Thinking, I guess, that no one had seen us, I backed up, course-corrected, and steered into the complex, eventually finding my own garage.[49] Just as I pulled in, a different neighbor ran over shouting, "You could have killed someone back there!"

"Get out of my garage or I'll kill you," I warned her. I was completely out of control.

While that woman went and called the police on me, I attempted to do the right thing by waking up the neighbor

---

[49] I had a hydraulic lifter on this car, which is the only reason I could get into my garage. Otherwise it wouldn't have been drivable!

whose car I'd wrecked. He and I had a good rapport; I knew his wife especially well. As this neighbor was older, though, he was already in bed. Unable to rouse him, I was almost back to my place when the cops showed up. "Stop right there!" the lead officer said. Belligerent, I ignored them, so they knocked me down, handcuffed me, and placed me under arrest. My charges were several, including DWI.

Terry called Jeffrey to let him know I was in jail. He did come to bail me out, but our reunion was brief and chilly. The next day, in July 1997, he sent me this email: "I really wonder why I spent Saturday night trying to get you out of jail. I have days, too, when I need someone's love, and I have just about given up on getting love back from you." I, meanwhile, wanted more love, too—so I went and adopted another dog, a female miniature schnauzer. (You'll recall that a person does stupid things in the depressive aftermath of X.) I named her Angel because she was an angel for alleviating my sadness.

Technically still married, Jeffrey and I were on-again, off-again through November 1997. At that point, he talked me into selling the Newport Beach flip-house (clearly, I'd never gotten around to flipping it) and move in with him full-time to the newly-rehabbed Beverly Hills house. "You obviously enjoy LA more than Orange County," Jeffrey said, "so why not just live there with me?" He made a good point, but his motivations ran deeper. Jeffrey blamed Lance and Pat for bringing me with them to Newport Beach, and he wanted them gone from my life going forward. Getting rid of the Newport flip-house meant getting rid of Lance and Pat, too—good friends to me, but bad men to my husband, who had tattled on him and cost him a Mercedes.

This is the kind of shell game that billionaires with unlimited funds like to play. What Jeffrey couldn't have predicted was how many "new friends" would take their place in LA.

Settlement Deal

Because Jeffrey still had a foundation to maintain back in Salt Lake, four kids to visit, and several other properties to keep up around the country, our "full-time" arrangement in Beverly Hills was anything but. It changed month to month depending on Jeffrey's schedule. Sometimes we spent two weeks of the month together, sometimes two days; and less and less toward the end of our relationship.

Bored out of my skull at twenty-seven years old, I found creative ways to keep busy. I traveled to Texas frequently, buying luxury used sports cars from Enrique Cruz that I knew were in high demand in LA, driving or shipping them to California, and reselling them at a profit. While I made good, honest money this way, it was the work—the productive outlet of it—that attracted me more than the money. I didn't need the money. I was still netting half a million dollars a year on Jeffrey's payroll every year.[50] What I needed was a challenge, a distraction in the absence of his affection. So what if it took me away on Jeffrey's rare day off. So what if he complained *I never see you anymore, Paul.* Let him accommodate me for once. I wasn't just my father, looking for someone else to foot the bills, and I wasn't just my mother, intent on working herself to the bone and resigned to the middle class. I was the product of them both: a young man confused about how to be industrious, while also letting someone love me. About how to be responsible, when LA's party scene beckoned seductively.

---

[50] It was important to Jeffrey that I be well-provided-for, as evidenced by a February 1998 letter in which he wrote: "I will not abandon you financially." This statement was a deeply felt promise to always take care of me. That he reneged on this promise a few years later doesn't matter. I wasn't with Jeffrey because he was my sugar daddy. I was with him because I loved him—my partner and my husband.

Rather than spend a ton of time dwelling on these tensions, I began having all-night parties whenever I was at the Beverly Hills house and Jeffrey was gone. I'd go out and shut down the bars, then invite twenty or thirty people to come home with me and keep the party going. There'd be plates of cocaine all over the house, and guests dancing to "Everybody (Backstreet's Back)" on the countertops in high-heeled boots or swimming naked in the pool. Jeffrey would send his minions to cruise by and report on the number of cars in the driveway before interrogating me the next day about where and with whom I'd been. Hurt, and therefore spiteful, his messages became passive-aggressive. "I like having dogs," Jeffrey typed in a fax delivered April 1998. "They are consistently loving and they don't lie." Recalling my warning, from the days of the Wilshire condo, that he respect my boundaries, such "reproaches" were the most "action" Jeffrey ever took against me. Until, that is, the summer of 1998, when he showed up unannounced at one of my by-now-infamous house parties, and threw everyone out without apology.[51]

"Paul, I can't go on like this," Jeffrey said, once the last stragglers had cleared out. "You've been taking advantage of my love for you. I think it's best you find a place of your own."

As a "settlement deal," he pledged to give me half the value of the Beverly Hills house, which after our extensive renovations, amounted to $2.1 million. "I'll give it to you over time," he said (as doing so would be easier to explain to his accountants), "beginning with purchasing you a house to move into now. Where do you want to live?"

Chris Brown—he of the "Hey, girl!" notoriety, who'd scandalized my mother—referred me to a real estate agent,

---

[51] The parties were destructive. I'll admit that. I'll also admit here that Chris Brown had moved into the Beverly Hills house with me, and brought along his two chew-happy bulldogs, who proceeded to gnaw on all the baseboards. Jeffrey had every right to throw everyone out, including Chris. The dogs were really the last straw.

who worked with me to find the best place to live in LA. After weeks of looking, I decided on a house in West Hollywood, only a couple of miles from the Beverly Hills house. Jeffrey kept his end of this part of the deal and bought it for me, wiring $550,000 to the seller but putting the house in my name. He also purchased for me the last car he ever would: a new 1999 Mercedes SL to replace my "old" '97 SL. Valued at $100,000, the car brought the total of what he had given me to $650,000, leaving a balance of $1.45 million, payable in installments (the specifics of which were to be determined at a later date).

I was sad about the end—and this time, I knew for sure it was The End—of the first real relationship I'd ever had. Jeffrey, it should be noted, did not think it was The End, not until I sued him. More on that soon. On another level, though, it felt liberating. Finally, I had the freedom to do as I pleased without having to feel guilty or worry about what Jeffrey would think. I no longer owed him anything, not my loyalty or my love, and as a result, he had nothing with which to control me.[52]

I should have applied the brakes at this juncture, slowing down to take stock and reevaluate my life. Instead, I put the pedal to the metal, accelerating much faster than even a Mercedes SL could go.

Floodgates of Promiscuity

They say it takes roughly half the length of a relationship to get over that relationship once it dissolves. All told, Jeffrey and I had been together for nearly five years, so by that math, I could

---

[52] Sad, liberated, but grateful, too. I want to make sure I include that last. In July 1998, Jeffrey wrote: "I gave it a shot and didn't hit the mark. But I think we both learned a lot. Maybe that counts somewhere." If I didn't tell you then, Jeffrey, it totally counted. Thank you for loving me, and teaching me everything you did.

have used a good two-point-five years to process. But then I met Robert Franklin.

Me with Robert, out for a night on the town in
West Hollywood circa 2000.

If ever I have experienced love at first sight, it was with Rob. A mutual friend introduced us, and instantly I was smitten by Rob's blue eyes, his gorgeous smile, a height and build that mirrored mine exactly. As he was only eighteen, it must have been like what the twenty-years-my-senior Jeffrey had felt upon meeting me. *Here's someone fresh. Young. Breathtaking.*

I want him.

We started seeing each other almost immediately. Head over heels, I thought I'd never been as into someone as I was Rob. I wanted to know everything about him: his dreams, his fantasies, his family dynamics. Rob was the much-loved child of two moms—a lesbian couple who'd raised him to seek out and embrace the beauty in each person. *How amazing it must have been to grow up in that environment,* I marveled, *as opposed to the promise of fire-and-brimstone damnation!* I liked Rob's moms at once. But not as much as I liked their son—beautiful, perfect Rob. Young and uninhibited, he loved to party and could go all night, so go all night, every night, we did!

Guess what happens to fires that burn that hot? Yeah. They flame out way more quickly, having used up all the fuel at the beginning. Soon, my wandering eye noticed the veritable buffet of enticing options populating the WeHo (West Hollywood) landscape, and I knew I couldn't remain faithful, not even to one as delicious as Rob. The weight of my failed five-year relationship still hung heavy around my neck; to throw it off, I needed to properly rebound, to do what Young Paul had never had the chance to do: sow my gay oats! A few months after meeting Rob, I told him: "We need to take a break. I want to be able to date other men without cheating on you. I know that sucks to hear, and I'm sorry, but it's the truth."

Understandably, Rob was hurt. But I think, on some level, he also appreciated my honesty—because we somehow managed to stay best friends. Which meant that I kept (almost) all the perks of having devoutly monogamous Rob in my life, with none of the drawbacks.

That dirty work done, and with a triumphant roar, I threw open the floodgates of promiscuity. WeHo was and still is the gay district of LA, itself the second-gayest city (after New York City) in the country. With very little responsibility[53] and lots of time and money on my hands, I started going out every night and sleeping around, taking three or four partners a week (if not, on occasion, per night). It was exciting, sure, but it was about more

---

[53] While I continued to write letters and emails home, and call Gramaw Green to check in, it was apparent our lives had diverted down totally different tracks. Her cards to me, once the thing I'd lived for in Germany, seemed quaint in comparison to my high playboy lifestyle. "Well," she wrote, in a letter from Summer 1998, "I don't see what you miss by [not] being in McAllen. There's [sic] no jobs for people without college or no professional experience. You have to be older and in politics to get a good job and belong to a large family so you can bring the politicians lots of votes. That's the game." The "game" in LA, meanwhile, was How Many Men Can Paul Seduce?

than the thrill of the chase. Sex (even, and especially, sex with strangers) was validation. For ten to twenty minutes at a time, it filled the empty void I still nursed from childhood and my early adulthood, when I tried over and over again to earn my family's love and acceptance, and each time been found wanting. Now, every man who chose to sleep with me was, I convinced myself, choosing *me*, whether or not we saw each other again, or ever spoke. Sometimes the sex was so anonymous I didn't catch his name or even hear his voice. It was enough to know that he (or they, if multiple bodies were involved) desired me.

I never felt bad about what I was doing because "being safe" had been so deeply drilled into my head that even when I was drunk or high, I always, always used condoms.[54] And the fact that I was technically single meant no guilt, because who was I hurting? No one!

We met at bars and clubs, parties and bathhouses. Money got me into these circles, and the easy way I said Yes to everything and everyone kept me there. I bought all the drugs, did all the drugs, shared all the drugs[55] (including, occasionally, meth[56]—

---

[54] Usually, I was the top, so I controlled whether or not we used condoms. On the rarer occasion that I received, I insisted my partners wear condoms. It was a no-brainer; all around us, people were dying of AIDS. You'd see them on TV or in the newspaper with their lesions. If something as simple as a piece of latex could protect me, I was all for it. This single precaution is probably why my mother will never have to watch me die of AIDS.

[55] GHB, alternated with coke, had become my party drug of choice. Unlike alcohol, there was no way for law enforcement to test for GHB then, so if I got pulled over, it appeared as though I was sober.

[56] I know what you're thinking here. Isn't that dangerous? Isn't meth addictive? Yes—but I only did meth when there was no coke, and I never did either one without combining it with a downer like alcohol. I was too sensitive to uppers otherwise, which mimicked the symptoms of a panic attack. Meth and coke helped me "keep

which I can tell you, makes you want sex like nothing else. You're insatiable on meth, taking as many partners as you can get for as long as you can get them. Many friends contracted HIV this way). A high point (pun intended) was getting invited to a party at Madonna's brother's house. It was Halloween and I went in drag as Farrah Fawcett. While I didn't get to meet my pop idol, it was still cool to do lines with her brother in the bedroom, before rejoining the masses downstairs.

Two decades later, my sister Joy would observe how my behavior during this time—specifically, the way I chased men—imitated that of our mother. It was on a different scale, certainly. Where Mom didn't date more than a handful of men over the years, and my conquests numbered in the hundreds, if not thousands, Joy was right that my mother and I got the same things out of it: namely, attention; feeling wanted; feeling loved. If Mom could find that in one man, though, she was satisfied, while I needed another one, and then the one after him. I never expected, or wanted, them to stick around. In fact, it was better if I could move on to the next one right away, because that was one more person, in this twisted numbers game, to validate my existence. I felt popular, and determined to make up for my lonely, confused adolescence.

Too Much Traffic

In the fall of 1998, I went home to Texas for a visit. Mom was now living in a duplex in Austin that we'd bought together after she'd decided to upgrade from her previous digs. The duplex

---

the party going" when I was tired but not ready to go home. On their own, they made me freak out, which is why I never developed a dependency on them. It's hard to get addicted to something that makes you feel so uncomfortable in your own skin.

had about two thousand square feet of space on each side. She lived in one side and rented out the other; with that income, she paid for her living expenses (minimal, as I'd paid off her car) and invested the rest. Whatever the stock market yielded, we agreed, would be mine. I'd long ago satisfied the mortgage and never really expected to see a return on my investment. It was more of a gift to my mother, as I loved her and had myself been so abundantly blessed.

On this visit, however, Mom expressed a desire for a different house. She was tired of going up and down the stairs, she said. "And it's not just the stairs. It's also Austin. The city's getting too big," she complained. "There's too much traffic." Would it be okay if she mortgaged the duplex so she could buy a new house in San Marcos, thirty miles south of Austin? "I'll still manage the duplex from San Marcos," she promised. "Nothing about our partnership will really change on your end."

"That's fine, Mom," I said, "if that's what you want."

She then suggested I "sell" her the Austin duplex, so that it was in her name only. "It will make it easier for me to get a home equity loan," she explained.

Amenable, I sold her my interest for five or ten dollars—a piddling amount, just to make it all official—as, again, the duplex had been my gift to her. I wasn't trying to make money off of her. I didn't need it.

Once the duplex was in her name, she mortgaged it and paid cash for her new home in San Marcos, far away from the hustle and bustle of Austin. She rented out both sides of the duplex and easily made the monthly mortgage payment, with money to spare. Mom was happy. I was happy. What could go wrong?

As it turned out, everything.

It's a story for a later chapter, but it involves Las Vegas, Mom's new man, and suicidal ideation. No, the drama of my life never ends. It merely hibernates for a time, regaining its strength, so it can pounce.

12

Making Millionaires

Terry, the guy who'd messed with my rearview mirror the night I crashed the Mercedes, became my live-in roommate in the West Hollywood house. A hairdresser, he cut and colored his clients' hair (mine included) at the house, and I let him do it so long as he took care of Angel and looked after the house when I wasn't around.

The day I returned from visiting family in McAllen, Terry was doing a woman's hair at the WeHo house. "Judith Storm," she said, by way of introduction. She was petite, in her late forties or early fifties, with shoulder-length blond hair and blue eyes—in every way, the look of an "LA woman" in 1998. "Terry here has told me so much about you. I'm wondering if you'd be interested in an investment opportunity."

"Tell me more," I said. Back then, I was interested in anything that turned some money into more money.

"It's a portfolio company," Judith explained, walking with me into the next room. "Basically, they help up-and-coming businesses go public, so the businesses can make a bunch of money and expand. The key," she continued, "is getting in on the ground level, before they start the IPO process. Because once the businesses become super successful, everyone wants a piece of the pie—and by then, it's too late."

She went on to describe the "astronomical profits" awaiting the savvy investor, and how this company, Future Venture Capital, was looking for investors just like me. I'd done enough day-trading to know that, typically, when a business went public, its prices skyrocketed overnight. By buying and selling at the right times, I'd already made thirty or forty thousand dollars this way. But Judith was talking hundreds of thousands, potentially, depending on the size of the nest egg I put up.

"Would you be willing to meet with one of my associates at Future Venture Capital?" she asked. "He can tell you more about it and answer all your questions."

"Sure," I agreed, still hesitant at this point, but intrigued to hear more. If nothing else, I thought, I'd learn something valuable. Jeffrey had always handled the money in the past; all I really knew how to do was spend it.

At lunch the next week, Judith and her associate, Mason Wright, slid a slick brochure across the table. It highlighted all the businesses that Future Venture Capital then owned stock in, and advertised a guaranteed *triple* return on my investment within ninety days. "How much do people generally invest upfront?" I wanted to know.

"That depends on how much money they have," Mason said, "and how much money they want to make. What amount would be comfortable for you?"

What should I say? Ten thousand? Twenty? Hell, I had a lot more than that. "One hundred thousand," I said. "If you can turn that into three hundred thousand, I'll be pleased."

"That's a great start," Mason enthused, shaking my hand and already eying my checkbook hungrily. I wrote a check for the full amount like I was paying for groceries, not signing my wealth away to people I really knew nothing about.[57]

---

[57] Even though Judith was the one to rope me into the Ponzi scheme initially, today, I have no ill will toward her. She was a dingbat who

Million Dollars Cash

Shortly after that meeting, a man named Leo Schwartz contacted me on behalf of Future Venture Capital. He wanted to thank me for placing my faith, and my funds, in his company by flying me up to San Francisco to meet the C-suites of the businesses in the portfolio. "Oh, that's not necessary," I graciously declined. "I trust you. I'll just wait for the businesses to go public, and receive my portion of the dividends then."

"I insist," Leo said. "First-class airfare, accommodations at a five-star boutique hotel, all expenses paid. Please say you'll come."

Persuaded, I accepted. I didn't know it was a gimmick meant to tempt me into investing even more, or how most of my initial hundred thousand had already been divvied up—not among the pre-IPO businesses, but between those who secured the deal: Mason, Judith, and even my roommate Terry, who received a $10,000 "finder's fee" for turning them on to me.

A limousine blasting the "Nobody's Supposed to Be Here" remix by Deborah Cox picked me up on the morning of my flight, and dropped me at the airport, where I met Mason and Leo. As promised, the three of us flew first-class to San Francisco. They spent most of the flight grilling me about Jeffrey as the source of my money, no doubt wondering how much more they might squeeze out of him/me. I took their pointed questions to mean they were sympathetic to everything I'd been through, and honestly enthusiastic about seeing my money grow. At least, that's what their treatment of me (limo service everywhere we went; prix fixe meals with champagne) seemed to indicate. And we did meet with staff at several of the

really believed Future Venture Capital was trying to do some good in the world. I feel sorry for her, and everyone else she unwittingly conned.

businesses about to make it big—good people, who appreciated my "taking a chance" on them, and were already celebrating the money we'd all soon have. I left San Francisco a believer; I'd seen it all with my own eyes.

On the return flight home, and after a few drinks, Leo asked, "Paul: If I offered you two hundred thousand right now as a return on your initial investment, would you take it?"

"No," I said. "I'd rather wait the full ninety days to get my three hundred thousand." *Or more*, I secretly thought, convinced by everything I'd witnessed that I'd made the investment of a lifetime.

"Then what if I said you could purchase additional shares, right now, directly from the businesses you just met with, and make even more profit?"

"Well, Leo, I'd say that sounds like a great deal."

"Listen, Paul, I like you. You're a man of your word. You've already helped make so much possible for so many people. I'd like to see that generosity come back to you, in the form of more money."

Long story short, Leo proposed that he, Mason, and I start our own venture capital company, for the purposes of cutting out the middle men. "You could be the president," Leo said, "since you'd be fronting the seed money. But Mason and I would do all the work, and all you'd have to do is sit back and watch your money grow."

"How much are we talking?"

"I reckon it'd take a million dollars cash to get started," he said. "But with that kind of investment," he quickly continued, perhaps having noticed me blanch, "we'd all soon be wildly rich. *Wildly*, Paul," he emphasized.

Huh. Venture capital investing is pretty easy if you know the right people, I thought. I remember feeling smug. With the million-plus Jeffrey still owed me from our settlement deal, I'd make three million, and most likely more. How lucky was I?

All I needed to do now was convince Jeffrey to finish paying me off with one lump sum.

Doing Me a Favor

"That's not how venture capital works, Paul," Jeffrey said, exasperated, once I'd filled him in on the details of my plan. "If it was that easy, everybody would be millionaires."

He not only shut down my request, he told me to get out from under Future Venture Capital while I still could—while "all" I had "lost" was a hundred thousand.

"Bad news," I relayed to Leo, when next we connected via phone. "I won't be able to help you start the company. I don't have the money, and Jeffrey is refusing to give it to me."

"The bastard!" Leo cursed, incensed. He hung up, and was knocking on my door fifteen minutes later.

"We can't let him get away with this!" Leo came in yelling. "Jeffrey is just doing this to keep you financially beholden to him," he claimed. "That money is rightfully yours. Besides," he confessed, "I've already committed to buying the stock. We can't back out now."

"What do you suggest?" I asked.

"Do you have any assets you can cash in?" Leo asked. "You own this house outright, yes?"

"Sure, but—"

"Mortgaging the house, plus whatever you have in your money management accounts, should be enough. We'll liquify those—oh, and sell your second Mercedes, too," he said, "and that should get us close to one million."

"Wait a minute—"

But he was doing me a favor. That's how Leo put it. For "just" the $920,000 I could come up with between the home loan, my car, and my accounts, I would "never have to rely on Jeffrey for anything" ever again.

"Come on, Paul. Don't let Jeffrey do this to you." Sensing my reluctance, Leo then said, "The company will pay the mortgage on your house until you get all your money back, okay? We'll also pay you a monthly salary of ten grand, so you'll still have income and can go on with your life as usual. What have you got to lose?"

Everything, reader. I had everything to lose.

I contacted my financial advisor at Merrill Lynch, a young man to whom Enrique Cruz had introduced me. Earlier in the year, I'd given him four hundred thousand dollars to invest for me. "Hey," I asked him over email, "what do you think about this investment opportunity?" I sent him the prospectus for the initial hundred-thousand-dollar investment I'd made in Future Venture Capital, and told him a little about the new venture capital company I'd be helping to start, tentatively called World Wide Internet.

"It seems risky," my advisor wrote back. "But then, I don't have a lot of experience with venture capital. If you've seen the businesses and feel comfortable investing in them, then you should. It's your money to do with what you want."

To this day, I'm still shocked that he cashed out my entire account without so much as a *Let's see what your initial investment does first, no?* In November 1998, he wired the whole sum to an account Leo controlled, which got the ball rolling until my home loan could be approved. In the meantime, to keep me happy, Leo and Mason took me out to fancy dinners in the best restaurants, encouraged me to continue partying, and sent limos anytime I needed to go anywhere.

When my home loan came through in January 1999, World Wide Internet officially incorporated.

Snags

"Everything's great," Leo said, any time I checked in on the status of our new venture. "Stop worrying so much. Go to Mardi Gras. Have some fun."

As it was February, and time for my annual trip to Sydney, I went—for a month, and for the first time without Jeffrey. It was fantastic as always. Leo (using my money, I now know) paid for first-class round-trip airfare and the best suite in the city.

Upon my return, Leo said we needed company credit cards. "Since World Wide Internet is so new, and you have excellent credit, will you sign personally for the company? The company will of course pay the bills."

No problem.

Next, he said, we needed company cars. "If you'll lease them for us, then we can all have nice cars now. Once we go public, the company will pay the leases in full."

Okay!

We leased a car for Mason, one for Mason's girlfriend, and even a jeep for my roommate Terry.[58] Soon, we'd all be so rich it wouldn't matter, I thought. All I had to do was give these guys

---

[58] Terry was collateral damage. He got brought along on this ride simply because he knew and lived with me. I felt bad, until I learned that he, too, was stealing from me. He'd been pawning pieces of my jewelry to fund his meth habit, which I didn't find out about until I discovered the receipts one day. "I was going to pay you back," Terry said. "I just borrowed the money for some bills." I was about to call the police on him when Leo intervened. "We don't call the police on friends," Leo reprimanded me. "World Wide Internet will pay you back." They couldn't understand that it wasn't about the money; it was about them lying to me and using me.

money now; in return, I'd get way more money later. It never occurred to me not to trust them.[59]

Somehow, in the middle of everything going on, I made two final $100K transfers on the same day without realizing it. Combined with the "old" '97 Mercedes I'd already given Leo's girlfriend to drive, I'd effectively ceded the company not $920,000, but $1.1 million. No one corrected me.

As spring turned into summer, we hit a few "snags" with our portfolio businesses. "Nothing to worry about," Mason assured me, as he'd recently taken on some new investors, so there was plenty of money to keep operating. The bills were getting paid as agreed, so who was I to question anything?

"Now we should get new company homes," Leo announced. He and his girlfriend had been staying in an expensive Beverly Hills hotel. Leasing a house for them would be cheaper, he said—so I signed the lease on a $12,000 a month house in Hollywood Hills. World Wide Internet then purchased Mason's father's house in the San Fernando Valley for Leo's brother to live in, as the brother had become the treasurer of the company.

"Exactly how far away are we from going public?" I wanted to know. I was getting close to needing that big payday.

"Any day now," Leo assured me. Then: "Say, don't you have a birthday coming up?"

In August 1999, I turned twenty-nine years old. To thank me for making them all millionaires, Leo threw me my biggest party yet. He actually put me in charge of planning it (to keep me busy and distracted, no doubt), but World Wide Internet, he said, would foot the bill, which meant, in a nutshell, that I

---

[59] But also, when you haven't worked hard for what you have, you're not as apt to care about what happens to your money. There's no way that today my money would go to Leo as easily as it did then. I don't throw it around like there's an endless bank account anymore. It was a lesson I had to learn the hard way.

would be paying for my own party. Why didn't I see that? We rented out Club Rage, flew Paris and Johnny in from Australia, and in total, dropped thirty G on a stupidly decadent night. My birthday gift to myself was another schnauzer, a playmate for Angel named Johan.

Angel was my first schnauzer. I got her when I got my DUI in Newport Beach. Johan I got for my 29th birthday.

Determined to show just how solidly he was on my side, following this epic party, Leo suggested I meet with a prominent divorce attorney he knew. "Maybe you can get that money Jeffrey still owes you after all," he said. Leo was always looking out for me like that; what a good friend! According to this attorney, I had an "amazing" case against Jeffrey, based on the letter alone in which he'd written: "I will not abandon you financially."

Leo is right, I reasoned. *It's not fair of Jeffrey to withhold what he promised me.* I let the lawyer send Jeffrey a letter of demand. The law firm had already agreed to a hybrid pay scale, wherein they'd only bill half their normal fee and collect the rest upon resolution. World Wide Internet, Leo had said, would cover these fees. Only, instead of producing the cash upon receipt of the letter, Jeffrey responded by filing a suit against me in Utah. These were fighting words, I decided.

We went to war.

Man Up

Around this time, in late 1999, Leo made plans to oust Mason from the company. "He's getting too greedy," Leo told me. "We need to eliminate him now, before we go public." He sent Mason and his fiancé to Hawaii under the auspices of a "wedding gift" trip, since they'd soon be getting married. While Mason was gone, Leo cleaned out Mason's office as though he could simply scrub him from World Wide Internet's record books.

When Mason returned, he asked to meet with me. "You need to know what Leo has been doing," he said. I figured he meant to tell me about Leo kicking him out, but it was much, much worse than that. As Mason explained, Leo had lately recruited two new investors by promising to triple, as he had me, their initial seed money. Only, when the men showed up to their next meeting, one of them had brought his lawyer along—an attorney by the name of Dick Barber—and as it happened, this Dick knew Leo personally. He knew all about Leo's attempts, in the past, to defraud wealthy but naive people of their money (indeed, if you hadn't yet guessed it: Leo had never invested my money, but was using it to finance his lifestyle), and Dick warned the two new investors not to commit. As a result, and scared that World Wide Internet was on the brink of collapsing, Leo had begun the process of moving the company overseas, where Dick Barber couldn't touch him. That's why he was offloading Mason. "And why," Mason told me, "you'll be next, Paul."

What could we do? If we didn't stop him, Leo would soon be gone, and what remained of my money along with him.

"Dick Barber, the attorney, has offered to help us," Mason said. "Dick says we can still save the company, if we remove Leo and find some viable startups to recoup our and the other investors' money."

As president of World Wide Internet, the decision fell to me. Feeling like I had no other choice, I put the fate of the company in Dick's hands, and prayed he would deliver us.

Dick did get Leo out of the picture pretty quickly, but recouping our money took longer than estimated. All the while, Mason and I were paying Dick cash for his services, both from our personal bank accounts and with capital Mason was raising for the company. When nothing "happened," I suspected Dick was now the one scamming us, confirmed when we found out he'd been delinquent in paying the company's car, home, and office space leases—all of which we'd transferred responsibility for to him, though they were still in my name.

Beside myself with stress and looming financial ruin, I ran back to my dependable drinking buddies: coke and GHB. I went from "dabbling only on the weekends" to daily use, as I didn't know what else to do.

As for Jeffrey and me, I'll spare you the gruesome details. Suffice it to say, when he sued me, I sued him, interrogatories were filed for both parties, and it all became very messy. Once I accepted how Leo had been playing me to get Jeffrey's money, I dropped my suit and forgave Jeffrey everything. He'd been right not to dump a bunch of money into my fool's errand. While he later called to thank me for backing off, sadly, the damage was done. I'd effectively destroyed what trust may have remained between us, and by extension, severed any chance of a future relationship with him.

We stayed friendly; the emails back and forth would continue for years. Occasionally I'd get lonely, and admitting again I'd made a mistake, beg him to take me back. Without fail, Jeffrey would reiterate we were done. I was scared, you know, of life without him. He'd been there for so long, taken care of everything for so long—and I'd proven in the first few months of our separation how I couldn't handle myself or my finances. Call me naive, or gullible, but I wanted to trust people. I thought Judith, and Mason, and Leo had my best interests at heart, because Jeffrey always had, and I missed his guiding presence in my life.

When I got involved with Future Venture Capital, it seemed an easy way to triple my settlement money from Jeffrey and prolong the amount of time I could live off of it, without making any changes to how I was living. I see now it was too good of a deal to be true—I was trying to "buy" financial independence, and ironically, lost just that. By the summer of 2000, my bank accounts were bare. The WeHo house Jeffrey had previously paid off was mortgaged. I'd sold all my cars to fund World Wide Internet, our new company intended to salvage the parent company. Several outstanding car leases were in my name. I felt sad, betrayed, and downright stupid. *Depressed*, as my thirtieth birthday loomed on the horizon, wasn't a stretch.

At the same time, I'd learned some valuable lessons, which would, at age twenty-nine, finally make me "man up." Namely, that I, and only I, am accountable for my actions. Just like you, and only you, are accountable for yours.

People will use you for their own selfish ends. They will bleed you dry. They will break your heart. And you're going to want to blame them.

In the end, though, *you're* the one saddled with debt. Served with a lawsuit. Stuck nursing a bad drug habit. And the sooner you can face the music (ideally sometime *before* you literally send your life up in flames—because yes, this story gets worse yet), the sooner you can claw your way back out.

13

Back to My Roots

The story with which I opened this book—sex-crazed, high, and halfway to dead the night of my thirtieth birthday party? Yeah, it happened. Exactly like that, too. Firefighters dragged me semi-conscious from my BMW X5, where it'd rolled to a stop in the middle of Westwood Boulevard, and took me by ambulance to UCLA Medical Center. I spent my first two days as a broke, depressed, thirty-year-old single gay man in the ER, assigned a well-meaning nurse who condemned my "drug problem" and said my blood toxicity levels were off the charts. "We didn't expect you to wake up," she chided me. "We told your friends you probably weren't going to make it."

Terry, Enrique, Chris Brown, Lance, and Pat were all in the waiting room hoping for a miracle. They called Jeffrey, who was out of the country at the time, to let him know what happened. Apparently (though this is all second-hand), Jeffrey also spoke over the phone with the attending physician. "The cops," the doctor told him, "are waiting for a copy of Paul's bloodwork. He's still on probation from a DWI in '97. If they see any drugs or alcohol in his system, he'll be arrested." Rumor has it my ex-husband proceeded to wire some money to this doctor, who then made it all go away. *A seizure*, the final report read. *No illicit drugs present.* I was too out of it to grasp the finer details, and Jeffrey said he couldn't remember when I questioned him many years later.

173

In November 2000, I emailed Jeffrey this admission: "I've been dreading turning 30 since I was 24 and had just come out. I guess it's been subconscious, but I've felt that I wouldn't be young, cute, and as desirable. That fear, coupled with my financial situation, took me on one of the wildest, scariest rides of my life." I described the IVs, the respirator, the catheter they'd had me hooked up to, and how I'd been tied to the bed for hours because I wouldn't stop convulsing. It was a wake-up call, I confessed. I was ready to make some changes. Slow down. Reassess what I wanted out of life.

Platinum DVD

The most pressing issues needed addressing first. In late 2000, this meant helping Mason salvage what we could from World Wide Internet, and creating some new revenue stream to pay what we still owed. An opportunity soon presented itself, the likes of which I never saw coming. But I suppose, given my history in sales, it made sense; at any rate, I was good at it.

The boyfriend (Cole) of one of my friends (Steven) had started running a porn distribution company out of their home in Venice. Basically, Cole was buying porn DVDs from a wholesaler for a dollar a pop and reselling them for up to ten dollars each: an incredibly lucrative model. He'd often bundle ten to twelve titles together (for which he'd paid no more than twelve dollars) and sell them for as much as a hundred. Most of the transactions occurred on eBay—a legal outlet at the time, so long as you didn't have explicit covers. According to Steven, the business was growing, and Cole needed a business partner.

"For $12,000," Cole promised me, "we can buy enough product to expand. I guarantee you'll make every penny back and more." While I'd been burned by deals like this one in the past, something about Cole convinced me to invest. I tapped Mason's and my imploding venture capital company to shore up Cole's and my porn distribution company, which we called Platinum DVD, and the rest, as they say, is history.

Within a few months' time, Platinum DVD started generating enough income to cover all of our bills, including the ones World Wide Internet stopped paying. To keep up with demand, we hired my most recent boyfriend Robert, who commuted to the Venice "office" every day from LA. I liked stopping by there when I could because they had Eve's "Let Me Blow Your Mind" on a loop. Most of the time, though, I was preoccupied buying cars from Enrique in Texas and selling them in California. With the bills more or less on autopay, suddenly I had spending money again.[60]

Our steadily sinking ship of a venture capital company might have been saved if it wasn't for Dick. The lawyer we'd hired to staunch the bleeding not only turned out to be as crooked as Leo, but now he had the company credit card. I sent him the January 2001 statement, showing a balance due of $5,000, and the check Dick gave me to pay it bounced. American Express then called to verify a suspicious series of charges totaling more than $70,000. As it turned out, Dick fancied a porn star. He racked up the charges buying her studio equipment with which to make her movies. "No, I never authorized those purchases," I said. Not only did Dick threaten me with a lawsuit, he sent his lady friend's producers to threaten me physically. It would be the first of many suits brought against me by individual investors in World Wide Internet, who believed I should have known what was going on from day one.

---

[60] I wasn't pen-palling or emailing with too many people in 2000; I didn't have the time. But I did write some letters to myself—pep talks, really—about how I was going to be okay. "Look at all the things you're doing," they read. "You're a good person." I stored them in my safe, so I could go back and reread them whenever I got too down on myself.

I needed more money, this time to cover my defensive legal fees. Bryce, my old friend from the club scene, approached me about his "brilliant" business idea: manufacturing and distributing GHB (which since my initial exposure to it had become a federally scheduled and harder to source substance). It was, however, still possible to get our hands on GBL, a precursor that can be converted to GHB when mixed with a sodium derivative. "I have the lab and all of the ingredients," Bryce said, "except for the GBL. If you'll import it, I'll cook it, and we'll split the final product." Stressed and distracted, I wasn't thinking clearly; I agreed to his harebrained scheme. These were the days before internet shopping, and before Big Brother's online surveillance. Who was watching? How could we be caught?

It takes two liters of List I (but legal) GBL to make thirty gallons of Schedule I (illegal) GHB. I ordered the GBL from the Netherlands, had it shipped to the Platinum DVD office, then flew down to Texas to pick up a car. Steven (Cole's boyfriend) called me as I was driving the car back to Hollywood. "Where are you?" he asked, his voice garbled and crackling across the miles.

"I don't know," I said. "The middle of nowhere. Reception is spotty. What's up?"

"You just got a package from the Netherlands. What do you want me to do with it?"

"Hang on to it. I'll pick it up when I get back."

Steven was quiet for a moment. "When will you be back?"

Weird, I thought. *It's not like Steven to care so much.* "A couple of days," I said.

"Okay," he said, and hung up.

Two hours later, my phone rang again. An unknown number. I answered it.

"Paul," Robert said, breathless and panicky. "As soon as the UPS driver dropped off your package, a whole SWAT team stormed the place!"

"What?" I pulled over on the side of the road, so I could focus on what Robert was saying.

"They told me not to call you, that it was 'obstruction' and they would arrest me, but I had to, Paul."

I couldn't believe it. It seemed the feds knew a lot more about GBL than I'd given them credit for.

"Here's what you're gonna do," Robert said. "Write down the name and number I'm about to give you. This guy is my friend but he's also an attorney. You need to call him right now and retain him before you get back to LA."

I did as he suggested, then continued driving home to face the music.

It would be months yet before anything else happened; when it did, it looked like six or seven local police officers, *not* the feds, surrounding my house with guns drawn and arresting me on the spot. Allegedly, the SWAT team had expected to uncover a large drug ring at the end of my GBL rainbow. They didn't know what to do with a lowly playboy and his personal penchant for GHB. I made bail and awaited a trial that never came. We ended up negotiating with the DA: I pleaded guilty to possession (a misdemeanor), paid a fine, and completed a bunch more community service hours. After a few years' probation, it was like I'd never committed a crime.

Going Down and Cumming Out

By Spring 2001, I had attorneys in several states on my payroll. That's because many of the jilted investors in World Wide Internet lived outside of California, and their lawsuits had been filed in their states of residence. I maxed out my credit cards paying for everything, and just when I thought I'd hit rock bottom, the federal government got involved, too. The US Securities and Exchange Commission (SEC) served me a subpoena compelling me to appear in court on criminal charges related to Leo's Ponzi scheme. Because I was the president, it appeared I was the one responsible, never mind I'd lost more of my own money than almost everyone else combined.

Feeling like I had no one else to turn to, I reached out to Jeffrey. "Please, just meet with me," I begged. I thought if I could explain my side, perhaps he'd be sympathetic and help me. He was and he did—to the tune of $125,000—so long, of course, as I promised to pay him back. Grateful, I gave him my green diamond wedding ring as collateral on the loan. It bought me some breathing room,[61] at least in the short-term, but Jeffrey never let me forget I owed him. The letters he sent me from March onward detailed the balance of the checks he'd written in my name. "I will assume the loan starts today," his first letter read.

I coped the way I always did: by diving back into drugs and drag. Each of these was an outlet in its own way. Both allowed me to escape reality. Around this time, a porn director whom I'd met at a party, and gone on to work with through Platinum DVD, asked if he could rent my home out for his next film. Shooting would take two days, for which he'd pay me two thousand dollars, "and if you want," he said, "you can even be *in* the film"—as Vivian.

It sounded like fun. On the second night of the shoot, the director filmed a party scene that would make the cut in a gay porno eventually titled *Going Down and Cumming Out in Beverly Hills*. If you watch closely, you can see both me (as

---

[61] After maxing out my credit cards, even with Jeffrey's generous gift I couldn't pay off everything that was outstanding. I was forced to close the credit cards, and World Wide Internet officially ceased to exist. There was a settlement with the SEC. Dick didn't move on it, so we sued his attorney's malpractice insurance. That money was funneled back to the investors and paid off the rest of the company's major debts. End of story.

Vivian)[62] and Robert in drag in my living room. Our roles, as well as all of the other drag queens' roles, were non-sexual.

Shortly after my one and only adult film experience, I overdosed on GHB for the second time. In Summer 2001, I wrecked another car and ended up back in the ER. My body and brain stayed locked in a coma for longer this go-around, and when I finally came to, I understood that if I didn't get out of LA, I would die there.

I wrapped things up with Cole, transferring full ownership of Platinum DVD back to him,[63] and worked with Enrique to sell my remaining cars. The week Grampa Green turned eighty-one, I emailed Jeffrey about the blockage they'd found in his heart. "Doctors say he's too old for surgery ... so I'm planning on spending as much time with him as I can." If anything, it seemed like one more warning to stop taking for granted my health, my youth (surprise, surprise: thirty had *not* signaled the end of my life as a gay man), my pride. In the same email, I commiserated with Jeffrey over the end of his latest relationship. His response:

> You basically said I should just learn to enjoy life alone, as I am too intimidating to ever have a real love. No matter who I am with, he will feel inferior to me. That really hurt. I do not feel like I'm better than anyone. All I want is to be normal.

---

[62] Shout-out to Schuron here, my MAC girl and one of my bridesmaids when I married Jeffrey, who did my makeup on-set!

[63] While our joint venture was genuinely good for a time, Cole and I ended on bad terms. I found out he was paying himself more money than me, and sued him for the balance. My attorney told me Cole didn't have any money. "That's impossible," I said. But it turned out Cole was a man of the instant-gratification persuasion. He'd spent his money as quickly as he'd made it, and there really was nothing left. We wound up in mediation. I think I made a grand off the suit. Soon, eBay phased out its adult section. That was the death knell for Platinum DVD.

Normal, I thought. *That's all I've ever wanted, too.* But was what we were doing normal? Here he was, dating other people—and still pouring his heart to me when they walked.

I decided to take the piece of advice he offered me more than nine months before. "It may be good for you to move back to Texas for a while," Jeffrey had emailed in September 2000. He was right. It was time.

Me as Vivian with Schuron, sitting at a high-top table at Bricks Club where I originally met Jeffrey and also had my RuPaul birthday party.

An Auto Dealer Named Marc

On October 30, 2001, I hitched my '01 Mercedes E55 AMG to the back of a U-Haul (after an all-night party to pack the truck up, mind you), and hit the highway bound for Austin. Destiny's Child provided the soundtrack. This would mark the "off-road adventure" period of my life, when I left the easy familiarity of LA's party scene for the gravel riverbeds and verdant greenbelts of a brand new city—the one where my mother had most recently lived.

In the early 2000s, Austin was not yet the booming metropolis it would become. A smattering of tall buildings, not tall enough to be called skyscrapers, peppered the city skyline, and less than 700,000 people called it home (compared to more than two million today). While Austin has always been a liberal city, I experienced more harassment here than I did in LA, though these instances were isolated and usually minor— someone yelling "faggots," for example, as I walked out of a gay bar with my friends. I started carrying a small handgun, just in case (this is Texas, after all), and knowing I could use it if I needed to gave me back a small measure of confidence. Otherwise, I played it smart, never holding a boyfriend's hand or kissing him in public. The risks, at the time, didn't outweigh the rewards.

I moved into one half of the duplex I originally bought for my mom and that was now a rental property. It was a great solution, since it meant I didn't have to worry about a mortgage. I still needed money to live on, though, and as all of the money I made on the sale of the WeHo house went to paying my small army of attorneys, I started looking around for a job. The natural fit, I felt, would be something to do with cars. It was the type of work for which I was most qualified, not to mention the kind I enjoyed the most.

When I was checking out an auto auction one day, I met a gay auto dealer named Marc. We hit it off, and he invited me to hang out with him and his friends that night—a low-key "movie night" during which we watched *Queer as Folk*. At this gathering, I would meet one of my best friends to this day: David Whitfield, Marc's top salesmen and a man I'd recruit to work for me.

As Marc explained, he just signed a lease on a larger dealership space—too big, even, for him alone. "How would you like to rent lot space from me?" he asked. "You could use it to get your own dealership off the ground, and I'd appreciate the extra income, too." It seemed like a safe, smart bet—much safer than trying to build something from nothing in a place where I knew no one else.

"You're on," I said, shaking his hand. "Provided I get to use David, too."

Marc agreed: David would sell for both of us.

For startup cash, I emptied a couple of mutual funds I'd forgotten I even had. They totaled roughly thirty thousand dollars, enough to seed the initial inventory of Platinum Motors[64]. I used it to buy my first five cars, and when David sold those, five more. Pretty soon, we were outselling Marc on his own lot—and he had forty or more cars to our five! Part of it was my experience. I had a highly trained eye for quality used vehicles, so I never bought or sold any lemons. Second, my comparatively low overhead costs meant I could pay more for the cars initially. To Marc's never-ending frustration, I outbid him at auction many times.

He tried to compensate by putting new "rules" in place. *You can't compete with me on certain hot-selling models,* he said. *You can't stock more than two of these particular cars*—and later, *You can't stock cars X, Y, and Z at all.* When I refused to play along, he tried upping my rent proportional to the types and number of vehicles I was carrying. It was maddening. I've never responded well to micro-managers, and it became clear our partnership had run its course.

After several months of this power struggle, I'd made enough local contacts in the industry to find my own place. It needed to accommodate at least ten vehicles (by then, I was moving anywhere from seven to twelve cars a month), and if it was bigger, I planned to expand by leasing lot space to another dealer the way

---

[64] Yep, I kept the "Platinum" name from Platinum DVD. Why? It's the best, a top-tier metal. And I like the color.

that Marc had to me (which I did eventually do). I settled on a lot with room for thirty vehicles across the street from BMW of Austin. It came with a separate space in the back for detail work, plus overflow spaces for an additional five cars if needed.

The best part was that David followed me. Installing David as my general manager meant I never had to worry when I wasn't at the dealership. I trusted him implicitly with the credit card and the checkbook, to make decisions in my absence, and not to abuse that trust. I was lucky to have such a good associate and friend.

Being across the street from BMW proved to be very good for business, given that we often carried the same type of inventory. I'd begun buying wholesale cars in McAllen—great high-end, low-mileage cars—from responsible dealers who sold to me over the phone.[65] I no longer lost whole days to auctions, or risked coming back empty-handed, and still I had the best cars coming out of the South. Compared to BMW of Austin, Platinum Motors could be way more competitive on price. We simply didn't have the enormous overhead they did. Consumers would stop there to look at cars, then end up buying from us after seeing what we had and what we were charging.

If at any point in my life I was "living the dream," this was it: working hard, making money, blaring Janet's "All for You" on the boombox, surrounded by my favorite toys.

Wear Your Seatbelt

There was leisure time in there, too. Although I'd drastically scaled back my partying ways, I still went out on occasion for

---

[65] Pro tip: Buying the cars is where you make your money. If you buy them right, you will always make a profit.

a casual drink with friends. A couple times a month, we'd also do coke on a Friday night. Inevitably, I'd be hungover the next Saturday and David would take that shift. I stayed away from GHB, though. Even had I wanted it (which I didn't, since now that I'd turned my life around, I was happy and didn't need it), I wouldn't have known where or how to get it in Texas. It was nice being (mostly) sober and productive in Austin.

My family was happy to have me home, too, especially my grandparents. I hadn't lived in the same state as Grampa and Gramaw Green in ten years. The first thing I did was to replace their failing vehicle with a year-old Mitsubishi Diamante I picked up at auction in Dallas. It was easy to do, and it made me feel good, knowing for once I could help out my grandparents in their time of need. Both they and my mother were "dealing with" my homosexuality the same way the military had: via a strict Don't Ask, Don't Tell policy. As long as I wasn't waving it in their faces, they could "overlook" this character flaw of mine, and I reintegrated into the family as best I could. They still thought I'd meet a girl to fix me; I still hoped they'd accept me as I was. We were riding it out to see whose wish came true first. Even so, I'd be lying if I said it wasn't comforting to have a family support system back in place. Ever since Jeffrey and I had split,[66] it felt like I'd been going it alone. But now I was a Flamer again, I knew where I belonged.

---

[66] Jeffrey and I kept in touch over email. He rarely contacted me of his own volition, but would respond to my calls and emails when I reached out to him. I secretly hoped that once I showed him I'd gotten my shit together and turned my life around, he'd give us another chance. *Five years*, I told myself, *means something*. I stayed in touch with Robert for the same reason, even though by 2001 he was exclusively dating a man named Nick. "If you're happy, I'm happy

My sister Joy had her first child, a daughter she named Katy, in December 2001. Katy was born with special needs. The doctors said she'd never be able to walk or talk. We didn't even know how much Katy could see or hear. They gave her a year to live, but she ended up gracing our lives for fourteen. Mom quit her job to take care of Katy. Watching her with her granddaughter was a night and day difference. She didn't perpetuate old patterns with Katy, pushing her to fit a particular mold; she simply loved her, exactly as she was. I was grateful my niece was on the receiving end of that love, and happy to see how Mom had grown. But I couldn't help but feel a little sad, too. It seemed to be the way things worked in our family: each generation held the next generation's faults against them, but by the third generation, all was forgiven. Gramaw Green had treated my mother poorly, but loved me as close to "unconditionally" as anyone in our family ever had. Except for Aunt Jessica, anyway.

With my niece Katy in 2007.

for you," I wrote to him. But it did hurt a little. I truly believe love is forever; that you can't un-love someone you've loved so deeply.

In late 2002 or early 2003, we got some terrible news: Aunt Jessica had been diagnosed with pancreatic cancer. It's one of the deadliest types of cancer, yet Aunt Jessica was one of the healthiest and fittest individuals I knew (certainly, the healthiest and fittest of her siblings); how could this be possible? Fortunately, her doctors believed they'd caught it early enough. "We're hoping for a full recovery," they said. I'd heard the same thing from Dad's doctors, though, and look how that turned out. So it was with guarded hope that we waited for Aunt Jessica to make it through surgery, and for the medical staff to declare her in remission. When they finally did, my whole world righted itself again. Half of me was sure she was dying, sure we'd already had our last conversation or shared our last party. But no! My biggest cheerleader, my shoulder to lean on, survived to see another day. I couldn't imagine my life without her, and for a precious few years yet, I wouldn't have to.

All in all, relocating to Austin was looking like the best move I could have made. I veered off-road to explore uncharted territory, and was rewarded for my courage with a healthier, happier life. My business was successful. My family was closer than we'd ever been. Less clouded by drugs and alcohol, my body and mind were my own again. The only thing missing in my life was romantic love. But then, perhaps it was best I take a break from that, too.

You should never be afraid, when things aren't working, to reassess your options, and if the occasion calls for it, strike off in a radically different direction. Sometimes it's the only way to ensure a clean break, and the time and space to get your head right again. Just one word of caution, if I may: Wear your seatbelt. By virtue of their very unfamiliarity, the ditches and rocky terrain off-highway are a little more treacherous than the asphalt road. It's easy to hit your head if you aren't careful. And harder still to let old habits die.

14

Platinum Implosion

Between 2002 and 2004, I went out with a lot of guys. None of them evolved into anything meaningful. I kept a torch burning for both Jeffrey and Robert, should either of them change their mind and decide they wanted to try "us" again. Both were happily dating other people, though, and Jeffrey in particular let me know it in no uncertain terms. "I'm not the same person today that you were boyfriends with at Brick's," I emailed him on one lonely night. "I've been changing myself for the better (I hope) … I think some people would call that growing up."

"I've moved on," Jeffrey responded. "You should, too."

If only it were that easy.

Robert and I were still good friends, at least, and in 2004, I went to visit him in California. He was single at the time, a fact that may or may not have inspired my impromptu trip. Over drinks at an LA bar, I told him I still loved him. "It was a mistake to ever let you go," I said. "I'm sorry. Would you take me back?"

"Paul," Robert said, grabbing my hand across the table. His eyes looked so sad, I knew what he would say before he said it. "You still don't know what you want out of life. And to be honest: neither do I."

I understood. We remained best friends. While I didn't get to see Robert as often as I would have liked, whenever we did connect, it was like no time had passed at all. I was lucky to have him in my life.

Come March 2005, I decided to go to Australia for Mardi Gras. I missed Paris and Johnny, and I missed the carefree young man I always felt like when I was there. As a courtesy, I emailed Jeffrey to let him know I'd be attending. "I'm going, too," he wrote back. "Maybe we could meet up for a drink."

A drink turned into flirting, became going back to Jeffrey's hotel room. We were naked, making out, and about to have sex when he suddenly jumped up and said he had to go. "I'm late for a meeting," he explained. I didn't buy the excuse (since that's what it was: the first thing he could think of to extricate himself from the situation), but I accepted it. He was terrified of falling back into something that had hurt us both so badly; I couldn't blame him. After I left, I didn't see him again on that trip.[67] Between my friends and the scene, there was enough going on to distract me, anyway.

I spent the rest of 2005 growing Platinum Motors. I'd long ago filled the thirty-car lot, plus the overflow area, and I began to think about finding a newer, bigger lot.

Before one could manifest, a drag queen friend in LA (Jamie) invited me to the Screen Actors Guild (SAG) Awards. Held annually since 1995, the SAG Awards honors the best in film and television achievement. Excited to go, I asked if I could bring some friends from Austin with me. Jamie couldn't get them tickets, he said, but they were welcome to visit California. Five guys from the original *Queer as Folk* screening party back in 2001, who'd heard many of the stories from my WeHo days and were curious to see the place in person, said they were in. We all flew out in early 2006. While I accompanied Jamie

---

[67] I did, however, email him one more time, with a plaintive, "Do you think we'll get it right in this lifetime? Or must we wait until the next time around?" Jeffrey didn't respond.

to the January 29 event at the Shrine Exposition Center, my Austin friends went out in LA. We planned to meet up as soon as the awards show was over.

The best-laid plans, right? I started drinking before the SAG Awards, drank throughout the event, and then went to an afterparty (held at someone's condo in WeHo) with Cole's ex-boyfriend Steven—where of course the partying continued. I didn't drink alcohol at the party because there was GHB, and having not indulged in that particular drug in five years, it seemed like high time to give it a go. When the liquid GHB mix came my way, I took a swig. When it came around a second time, I did a little more, never mind that it was still close to my last drink of alcohol to be dosing GHB twice. I felt great! Why, I wondered, had I ever quit?

You'll notice a running theme here, but "the last thing I remember before blacking out" was trying to hit on some hot bi guy (more of a challenge, and therefore more of a turn-on) in one of the bedrooms. "He just fell face-first onto the floor," the guy said, when Steven asked him what had happened. "Now he won't wake up!"

Steven carried me into the shower and tried to shock me back awake. The cold water did nothing for me, so he checked my pulse: weak and slow. "Hurry!" Steven said. "Bring some crystal!" He dipped his finger in the meth, then rubbed it under my tongue, hoping that would bring me back. Nothing. He tipped some up my nose. I started vomiting. Laid out as I was on my back, they rolled me onto my side so I wouldn't aspirate my own puke. I didn't wake up, but my heart rate and breathing returned to normal, and after a few hours, I did come to.

At first, I had no idea where I was—only that Missy Elliott's "Lose Control" was still pulsing in the background, and everything inside me felt *bad*. The crystal had finally kicked in and my previously sluggish heart was racing. I went from almost dead to trying to tear my own skin off, convinced that bugs were crawling all over me. Steven tried to calm me down, and to hide my freak-out from the party hosts, but pretty soon we were asked to leave. Someone used my phone to call David Whitfield, my partner from Platinum Motors and one of the Austin friends we were supposed to have met up with earlier.

The five of us were scheduled to fly out at noon that day, but when David came to get me, I was in no shape to fly. He insisted I sleep it off. He took me to a hotel, where I slept the rest of the day and all that night, too. Having sent my friends on ahead of me, he stayed by my side and watched over me, lest I again try to choke on my own vomit. Although I spent most of those twenty-four hours unconscious, I remember them as the worst of my life. The utter, whole-body sickness I felt every time I woke up was enough to send me retreating into the blackness again, until my poor, overworked organs had processed enough of the chemicals to let me come down.

At which point, I awoke to a harsh reality: *Robert was right.* I'd made some pretty big strides in my life, but when it came down to it, I still didn't know what I wanted. And because I didn't know what I wanted, I'd been willing to throw it all away on a party.

The LA lifestyle, I decided, had to be over for me forever. No more 'casual' hardcore partying, however infrequent. No more 'dipping my toe' back in the murky waters of GHB. Ever.

I was done.

At First Blush

Following my third and final overdose, I threw myself into work. Now was the time to see just how big Platinum Motors could become. James (the dealer who'd been renting from me) and I had already decided to go into business together, 50/50. We just needed the perfect lot for the company's next evolution.

On a tip from another dealer, James and I paid a visit to the owners of a large highway frontage lot. Buford and Gertrude Hogg were selling sixty-plus spaces and an on-site repair shop—enough room to accommodate our combined inventory, as well as work on our own and customers' cars. At first blush, everything seemed ideal.

"Why are you selling?" James wanted to know.

"We're ready to do restoration[68] work only," Buford said.

"And we don't need such a large space for that," Gertrude added.

"But have you been successful in this location?" I asked.

"Oh, yes," Gertrude said. She wheeled over to the desk in her wheelchair[69] and pulled the previous year's tax return from a drawer. "Take a look. Sixty thousand dollars a month, give or take."

James and I scanned the document.

"Really," Buford chimed in, "with your existing business, I think you could do $100 K a month easy. The potential for income here is endless."

We looked at each other, weighing the other's reaction.

"How much do you want for it?" James finally asked.

"A hundred thousand dollars down. We'd finance the other $900,000 ourselves. Save us all closing costs."

"Thanks," James said, betraying nothing about what he was thinking in speech or manner. "We'll let you know."

---

[68] He meant on Bentleys and Rolls-Royces, specifically—the highest of high-end restoration jobs, which would have allowed the Hoggs to still make a living.

[69] Adding insult to injury, I'd later discover that even Gertrude's "disability" was a sham. She only pretended not to be able to walk.

The four of us shook hands, then James and I huddled up in the parking lot.

"What'd you think?" I'd already made my mind up; I wanted the place.

"I'm interested," he said, "but my mom gets the final say." She would be acting as James's bank for his half of the down payment.

Later that week, James's cowboy-boot-wearing, pistol-toting, badass of a mother declined to invest. She'd been to see the property, she said. "It's a junk yard."

I looked again at the lot through her eyes. Yes, the Hoggs had done all of the construction themselves, and it showed. The "dealership" consisted of three trailers fastened together side by side. The shop and detail bays were simple metal structures of poor quality. An empty hole near the road had been waiting to be plugged with a new sign for years. I saw all of that. I also saw potential. With all the money we'd be making, we could upgrade the place properly, I thought. We could install a big, well-lit sign in that hole—one worthy of a million-dollar car lot!

"Sorry," James's mom reiterated. "I can't see it."

With my partner out of the picture, I met with the Hoggs a second time. "I'm still interested," I said, "but I don't have the full down payment."

"How much *do* you have?"

"If I refinanced my duplex, maybe sixty grand."

Buford and Gertrude conferred. "We like you, Paul. We'll do it for sixty. Go ahead and start the refinancing process, and we'll send you the paperwork as soon as we draw it up."

I was so happy they were willing to work with me, I didn't get any type of professional advice or bother to verify their financials. This was it. This was how I'd make a name for myself. At thirty-six, I finally knew what I wanted.

A Bottomless Money Pit

Once I had my expected fund date, I got with the Hoggs to review their paperwork. For thirty days after closing, the contract specified, Buford and Gertrude would stick around to help me get Platinum Motors up and running in its new location. They would let me keep their secretary, sales guys, and detail person. They would also help me find a mechanic, since Buford had been doing that work for them. In return, I agreed to assume their existing inventory: fifteen used Jaguars, all three to four years old, with V-8 engines. Not a problem, since I'd already applied and been approved for a $500,000 line of credit through my usual floor planner.[70] "Everything looks great," I said, signing where they indicated.

Shortly after I took over the business, the Hoggs' secretary told me how it really was. "They weren't ever actually making the money they claimed to be," she said. "None of the buildings on the property were built to code, or even with permits— meaning they're illegal, and you'll probably have to tear them down. And that hole out front, for the sign? Yeah, the Hoggs sold their signage rights to an advertising company. That's the other billboard you see out there. As the city only allows one sign per business, you can't put one in for Platinum Motors."

These were hard revelations to swallow, but not unmanageable. I knew going in that the buildings required updating, and once I did that, surely I'd bring in more money. Then eventually, I'd have enough to buy the signage rights back. Yes?

---

[70] A floor planner is a type of specialty lender that issues short-term loans to retailers (like auto dealers) to buy inventory. You can use them to purchase cars at auction, from individuals, from other dealers, or from banks that have repos. The loans get repaid as the items are sold.

No.

Forget the shoddy work the Hoggs had done to their buildings; apparently, Buford applied the same level of care to his customers. Soon, the list of former customer complaints I'd fielded—everything from "repairs" that hadn't fixed anything, to work they'd been charged for but that had never been completed—grew longer than the list of things wrong with the property. I could never hope to right all the Hoggs' wrongs and still end up ahead, let alone with surplus left over for improvements.

Worst of all, the Hoggs' crookedness extended to their employees. With the exception of the secretary, I had to fire every last one of them. David, my old general manager, came and worked with me for a time, but the lot was just too much for the two of us. We went through multiple mechanics trying to find someone reliable, struggled to meet the monthly mortgage payments, and lost money on every used Jaguar the Hoggs had deeded us. My baby was a bottomless money pit!

To blow off some steam, I drove to Dallas one weekend to meet up with some friends. We went to an all-night party at a downtown loft where, true to my word, I drank but did not take GHB. It didn't matter—I still wound up at the doctor's! One of my friends was horsing around, and smashed on tequila, picked me up, only to immediately fall over with me in his arms. What stopped our fall was my head as it struck a concrete pillar. The fall also jammed my back, which I didn't realize until I was driving back to Austin the next day. With sharp electric sparks lighting up my middle spine, I went to the clinic as soon as it opened Monday morning. Fatally, they prescribed me Vicodin,[71] the last and most powerful piece of my would-be addict's puzzle.

---

[71] Interestingly, Vicodin works by depressing the nervous system and blocking pain signals to the brain—an unintended side effect of

I'd actually been on Vicodin (generic name hydrocodone) twice before. Sometime in the early 2000s I was home visiting family in Austin when I developed a pneumothorax, or collapsed lung (apparently, this randomly happens to tall, thin people with long necks). I was taking a shower at Mom's place, reached up to grab the soap, and suddenly felt like someone had shoved a hot poker through my back. It became very difficult to breathe, and after I'd dried off and dressed, Mom rushed me to the ER. Generally, a pneumothorax will spontaneously repair itself, but if it doesn't, they have to insert a tube into your lung and manually suck it back up into shape. Either way, it's very painful. Both on this occasion, and with my second pneumothorax a year later, my lung managed to re-inflate itself. But they put me on Vicodin both times for the pain, and that's when I learned how great it made me feel: deceptively pain-free and full of energy!

Now on Vicodin for my back, I entered a vicious cycle. The harder I worked to get the dealership back in the black, the worse my back hurt. The worse my back hurt, the more opioids I took to dull it. The more opioids I chewed up and swallowed, the better I felt. The better I felt, the harder I worked—messing my back up further and never giving it a chance to heal. Soon, my stress levels peaked. I hadn't felt this bad since the venture capital investment scheme was imploding around me, six years before. Seeking an escape, I started partying again. I started combining alcohol, coke, and Vicodin, which I carried around with me at all times in a backpack like most girls carry purses. I fell back off the wagon for the umpteenth time. Just when it seemed like all was lost, however, the most unlikely source would reach down to give me a hand up: yoga.

---

which is decreased anxiety. For the duration of my time on Vicodin (which would be years), my anxiety was significantly lower; but as I now know, it was merely masking, not alleviating, my symptoms.

Solitude in the Storm

Through the years, I'd kept in touch with some select friends from Salt Lake City. One of them, Elizabeth (Eric's blonde friend, who'd worn black patent leather body suits), had become a yoga teacher. When I described everything I was going through, she suggested yoga might give me some relief. *If all yoga teachers are as calming as Elizabeth*, I thought—the sound of her voice alone was therapeutic, and her touch, gentle and kind—*it's worth a shot.* "Let in the light, Paul," she encouraged me, "and the universe will love you back."

I started with once-weekly classes at my local gym.[72] Three sessions in, I'd already noticed a difference. Between the stretching and the breath work, my back felt better and my mind was quieter. For an hour at a time, I could be present to nothing but the moment, to the signals my body was sending me. It was a respite from the chaos. Solitude in the storm. I added a second class per week, and then a third. Elizabeth said she was thrilled for me. Still, I struggled to carry that peace with me to work.

Platinum Motors was falling apart. I had a lot full of V8s and high-end luxury cars now depreciating at record speed. As 2007 wore on, gas prices rose and consumers began forgoing "splurge cars" for Hondas and Toyotas. The floor plan companies that had financed my BMWs and Mercedes didn't care; they wanted their money yesterday. Finding a sustainable solution consumed me every minute I wasn't focused on pranayamas.

---

[72] Initially, I was attending a nearby branch of 24-Hour Fitness. As my practice deepened, however, I switched to an all-male gym that offered a nude men's yoga class. Having been a skinny little guy with body image issues my whole life, it helped me to be surrounded by a variety of body types from fat to thin, old to young, and of all ethnicities. Not only did I become more comfortable in my own skin, but I learned to let go of my judgment as well.

And then—a beacon from the shore! A bank in McAllen with whom I had a long and positive history offered me a one-million-dollar line of credit. The idea was to pay off all the floor plan loans, effectively consolidating multiple high-interest notes into one lower-interest loan. The bank needed collateral, though—specifically, $100,000 in a CD. I'd already leveraged the duplex for the dealership down payment. The only other way I knew to get that kind of money quickly was Jeffrey.

Jeffrey and I were still in contact, and on friendlier terms since he'd started dating another twenty-something. He'd recently bought the boyfriend a Bentley, only to discover him in bed with his other boyfriend. Gathering my resolve, I called Jeffrey and explained the situation, saying, "I wouldn't ask you if I had any other option. I'm about to lose everything I've built."

"Give me a day to think about it," Jeffrey requested.

"Of course. And Jeffrey? Thank you."

Please, I prayed. *Please let Jeffrey help me one last time. Please help him see that Platinum Motors is different. It's honest. It's real. It's mine. I want it to survive.*

A week passed; nothing. I called. Left messages. Sent emails. Why wasn't Jeffrey getting back to me?

Several days later, he finally answered my call. "After careful consideration," Jeffrey said, "I've decided I just can't do it. I'm stretched too thin, money-wise, right now."

"Oh," I said, dumbfounded. *Last month, you bought your boy toy a $200,000 vehicle, and now you're stretched too thin?!* I didn't say this, but I sure as hell thought it. I wished he would have told me the truth: He wanted out of his promise to never abandon me financially.

Scared and frustrated, I sought legal counsel. Most of my problems stemmed from the Hoggs' false representations. Maybe I could be compensated that way? The attorney I hired agreed. "First, though, we'll need to file a reorganizing bankruptcy," she said, "to put all the creditors at bay and figure out a game plan." That move came with its own costs: namely, a $12,000 retainer.

I turned to my mother. While she didn't have the cash, she did have an unused credit card. I could charge the retainer to it, she said, and pay her back as I was able. That satisfied, we filed in Summer 2007. The dealership stayed open, but as the McAllen bank wouldn't allow me to purchase new inventory, only sell off what I'd already acquired, Platinum Motors' revenue plummeted, and I had to let all of the staff go. Dear, sweet David stayed with me until the end, when we changed the bankruptcy from reorganizing to final and discharged everything in November 2007.

The dealership (which they got back, by the way, after I ran out of resources with which to fight them)[73] wasn't Buford and Gertrude Hoggs' only victim. Having personally guaranteed all the loans and notes, I had to file for bankruptcy, too. And I took it personally, the death of a dream I'd worked so hard toward. I felt alone in my pain and disappointment. Cut off by Jeffrey. Stupid for having been deceived *yet again* by people I'd so earnestly trusted. It would have been easy to give up here. To turn my back on a world that had definitively turned its back on me.

But you can't do that: stop trusting everyone because a few rotten apples have abused your trust. You can't, because humans weren't designed to live in isolation. None of us can do it by ourselves. We need other people to pick us back up, to kiss our boo-boos, to say everything will be okay. If we didn't, we wouldn't read books about other people's experiences!

We also need to be better about incorporating self-care practices, and slowing down when we need to. It's how we find our way back to the open road.

---

73 I wanted so badly to burn it to the ground. But then they would have gotten to collect the insurance on the property, and I probably would have added arson to my already long list of legal infractions, so showing the greatest of self-restraint, I refrained.

15

My Two Brightest Stars, Gone

In the midst of my devastation, my yoga teacher friend Elizabeth let me know about a yoga teacher training and retreat happening in the jungles of Costa Rica. "It's in Nosara," she said—a tiny village on the Pacific Coast. "Thirty days. No TV or other distractions. Intensive Vinyasa flow. You'd do nothing but eat, sleep, and drink yoga; get your mind and your body healthy again. What do you think, Paul?"

I thought it sounded like precisely the thing I needed. Yoga was the only remaining still spot in my otherwise insane life. A chance to recoup in a peaceful and healing environment? Sign me up. And if I came out of it with a new career opportunity, too? So much the better!

The training cost money, of course, and there was an international plane ticket to buy, too. Amazingly, Mom agreed to add these to the credit card she was keeping for me, which I was then paying off at a ridiculous rate of something like fifty dollars a week. Using her card, I paid for the course, booked a ticket, and left the country in November 2007. General manager David was kind enough to stay behind and tie up the last loose ends at Platinum Motors[74] while I ran into the open arms of my future.

Our Delta flight left Houston at six in the morning, and touched down in Liberia before noon. Liberia was (still is) the smaller of Costa Rica's two airports, and looked more like an oversized hangar in those days than an international hub. It was open-air, with giant spinning ceiling fans and no security other than a customs agent who stamped your passport. Literally, cows and birds had to scramble off the runway as we landed. I remember listening to "Sweet Escape" by Gwen Stefani on my iPod and feeling my heart seize up at that point, like *What the hell have I done?* Far from a sweet escape, we'd very clearly just arrived to a Third World country. Could I handle it? Was this the solace I sought?

Don't ask me how I found where I was supposed to go next. Smart phones didn't connect us to everything and everyone then. Somehow, I got in a six-passenger van with approximately ten other riders and their luggage, and suffered through a fifty-mile drive to Nosara. Because it was the tail end of the rainy season, the roads were liquid with mud. Fifty miles took four hours to traverse. We almost got stuck several times, and the cloying humidity, which made it that much harder to breathe, did nothing to help my mounting anxiety.

It was beautiful, though. I'll give Costa Rica that much. Not even California is as lush and green as Central America's tropical forests. The trees were heavy with bananas, papayas, and passion fruit,[75] and my "alarm clock" every morning was

---

[74] The Hoggs actually broke into the dealership one night when I was in Costa Rica. They tried to take everything back before it was rightfully theirs again. In a last low blow to me, the cops ruled it was not criminal trespass.

[75] I'll admit here that I brought my own juicer to Costa Rica with me. It was the one "luxury item" I insisted on having, and I'm so glad I did. I'd already been juicing every day for years (my friend Steven had

the howler monkeys who passed through on their way to breakfast. The yoga "school," such as it was (consisting of two main pavilions and a kitchen) housed thirty students from around the US and Canada in private little casitas, each with a bed, a toilet, and a shower. They were spartan accommodations, but made naturally more luxurious by the outdoor abundance of pink and yellow flowers thriving in the daily downpours, and the beach just a five-minute walk away. At least we had electricity—lights and weak A/C.

Meeting the other students there for the training is when I really started to relax. All of them were cool (though I was the only gay man present), and like me, most of them were working through their own shit. We'd come for different reasons, but we hoped for the same outcome: a letting go of that which was no longer serving us; an acceptance of ourselves as perfect, just the way we were.

How often do any of us have the opportunity to stop? Listen? Learn? For four weeks in Nosara, I peeled back the layers of my conditioning—the "truths" about myself and my experience that I'd long ago convinced myself were gospel. I re-examined the evidence with fresh eyes, questioned everything about my ingrained belief system, and spent hours pondering what life and the universe actually meant. Little by little, I began to see there was nothing about Paul Flamer that needed changing or needed to be anything other than what and how and who he already was. Combined with the purifying physical practice of the asanas, the challenging mental study of Sanskrit, yogic history, and human

introduced me to it, as well as a superfood supplement), but in Costa Rica I didn't have to go to the grocery store; I simply walked to the stall on the side of the road and bought carrots that looked like mangoes, and other weird "ugly" fruits and vegetables you'd never see in an American market. And you know what? They tasted delicious. I attribute looking younger than my forty-nine years today (and retaining all of my teeth, despite the rampant drug use) to this regimen.

anatomy, and the uplifting traditions of group chanting and meditation, my whole life transformed in the space of thirty days. I stopped caring about what the wider world thought of me, what the church or my family expected of me. I fell in love with myself for the first time in my life!

RuPaul would have been proud.

The month concluded with individual student-led classes. I was scared to have to teach in front of everyone, but they told me I did well and would make a great instructor. At our very last group meeting, we went around and shared what we had learned. During my turn, I experienced a major catharsis. I cried uncontrollably as I described how much I'd grown. I thanked my new friends for facilitating my liberation (truly, the most empowering feeling I left Costa Rica with was one of freedom—specifically from the need to crucify myself, as though I wasn't worthy). We keep in touch via social media to this day, reminiscing about weekend river-rafting and horseback-riding excursions all those years ago, and holding each other accountable to keeping the "glow" alive.

Round Rock

Unfortunately, a "glow" does not a financially independent man make. Back in Texas, I had to start earning an income and figure out what was next for me. I knew I wanted to try teaching yoga, if for no other reason than to be perpetually surrounded by good vibes, but I wasn't sure that alone could sustain me. I picked up a couple of weekly classes at the gym I'd been attending before going to Costa Rica, and I also contacted Marc, the auto dealer for whom I'd previously worked in Austin. Given that he and I had parted on not such great terms, I assumed I'd find it difficult to work for him again, but now at least I had my yogic practice to ground me. *If things get out of balance*, I told myself, before accepting Marc's offer of a salesman position, *you can always quit.*

Teaching yoga, as it turned out, was far more stressful for me than taking yoga. Each class sent my panic-attack-prone self into a tailspin. I worried about everything. Was the room too hot? Too cold? Had I done both sides of a posture, or just the left one? (Thanks, dyslexia.) Were the sequences I strung together good enough? Thinking like this drove me crazy, and eventually led me to quit teaching yoga. The ironic part was how my students regularly complimented my style: "Your voice is so calming," they'd say. "You give an amazing class!" I thanked them for their encouragement, though what I really wanted to say was, "Are you kidding me?! I wish you could see inside my head right now!" Because inevitably, I felt sure I'd just taught the worst class ever.

Things at Marc's dealership didn't go much better. We clashed often and hard, usually over his micro-managing and constantly changing pay scale. I started to wonder if life would ever feel good again—easy and happy, the way it had in Costa Rica. One day, I was talking on the phone to Carla (my former condo-mate from Salt Lake City), and she invited me to visit her in Las Vegas. "I don't know," I said. "Las Vegas seems like the opposite of what I want right now. I'm looking to slow down, settle down, keep 'cultivating my inner peace.'" I smiled, knowing how hippie-dippy that sounded, and how at odds with the Party Paul she knew. But then, she, too, had "slowed down," having started a family and a full-time job.

"It's not like I live on the Strip," she said. "Well, just keep it in mind. My door's always open."

I did keep it in mind, but way at the back, focusing the rest of my brain power on salvaging my Austin-based existence. My back problems, which yoga had initially helped, had returned in full force. All of my disposable income was going toward getting massages. That's when I first considered massage school. *It's another great wellness tool*, I thought. *It would complement well my yoga practice.* Almost as soon as I began researching programs, though, I lost my tenant on the rented side of my duplex. Normally not a big deal, but this was 2008. The housing market had collapsed. No one could afford to live in the city.

Complicating this sudden drop in my supplemental income was the fact that re-financing the duplex to fund Platinum Motors had driven up my monthly payments exponentially. To compensate, I'd then stopped paying my property taxes, which meant I also owed back taxes. One day, I received a notice thanking me for my property tax payment. *What? Who paid this?* I wondered. *Was it Jeffrey?* That wouldn't have made any sense, of course—his name wasn't on the mortgage or anything—but that was the kind of rationale my mind still came up with sometimes: *Maybe he still cares about me!*

Anyway, it turned out the mortgage company had paid the taxes on my behalf, so I wouldn't default. Which was great, but I still couldn't make the mortgage. I needed a tenant, and in order to attract a tenant, I'd have to lower the rent so dramatically that I still wouldn't be able to make it. Not only could I *not* afford massage school, I was facing imminent homelessness. There was only one solution, I decided: I had to move out and lease both sides to make ends meet.

I loved that duplex and its convenient location to everything, but renting it out until the market recovered just made good sense. As for me, I moved into one of Pete's rental houses, in the North Austin suburb of Round Rock. Yes, my baby brother and his wife had since moved to Austin as well and bought a couple investment properties in the area. He made me a great deal for six months, so I could collect double rent from the duplex and hang on. I knew if anything went wrong—for example, if I lost another tenant and couldn't replace them—I'd have to sell at the bottom of the recession, and lose any equity I may have earned.

Over the next six months, I saved $10,000: enough to pay for massage school[76] *if* I didn't have to pay rent. When Carla said I could live with her for free (I'd never charged her rent in Salt Lake City, either), I found a massage school in Las Vegas and packed my bags for Nevada.

Heart Thing

Angel and Johan, my schnauzers, rode in the seat beside me and we towed only what would fit in a one-bedroom apartment. The truck I was driving (and over whose speakers I was spinning hip hop artist Neyo's "Miss Independent") wasn't even mine. It was owned by the bank, tied up in the bankruptcy claim my attorney said would take a few years to finalize. If dogs can sweat, all three of us did as a ninety-six-degree sun streamed in through the windows. September: not the best month to move to the desert. But it was the start of the fall semester, and the start of the rest of our lives.

After two days on the road, we pulled up to Carla's house: a single-story ranch she shared with two seemingly vicious dogs (the Rottweiler had immediately tried to eat Angel) and a screaming three-year-old. Off to a great start! Carla was ignoring all the madness, as she was at that moment on a work call. As in, she worked from home for an internet security company and *would always be around*. Also not very promising.

Scooping up Angel and Johan before they could die a butcher shop death in my absence, I stepped back aside and

---

[76] Most frustratingly, I realized around this time that I'd let a very significant part of my veteran's benefits lapse: namely, the GI Bill. Had I enrolled in massage school four years earlier, it would have covered my books and tuition and also paid me a living stipend, but I'd never even thought to use it. As it was, the benefit expired ten years after my discharge. I ended up taking out a student loan.

reassessed. Did I really want to do this? I even called my friend Amber from Texas, whose helpful opinion was: "What's your other option? Drive back to Texas and start all over here?" Touché. I started unpacking the U-Haul.

It took a few weeks, but eventually Carla and I found our groove again. Although her dogs Angel and Johan eventually got used to me, Carla really hated the sound of my juicer every morning. Once classes started for me, I kept busy studying and getting to know my new classmates. I discovered I had a genuine interest in massage, and I began to get excited about massage as a career. I also spent so much time on the table, getting free body work as we practiced on one another, that my back started feeling better, too. As a result, I was able to lift weights again at the gym for the first time in a while, though I also kept up with the yoga for "balance."

By November 2008, I was in the best shape, mentally and physically, of my life. My body had become so tanned and healthy, and I was physically so jacked I imagined it looked like skinny Paul's head had been photoshopped atop another's body. But I was genuinely happier, too. It must have shown, because when I went to visit Robert in California (he was then living in Hawaii, but staying with his Highland-based mothers for the Thanksgiving holiday), he commented on the apparent change in me. "You seem so different, Paul," Robert observed. "More focused, but also happier and more relaxed."

The last time I'd seen Robert was on a trip to Hawaii with his family in 2006. On that trip, I'd asked him again about the possibility of us getting back together, and he'd again graciously declined anything more than "friends with benefits." On this trip, though, when he expressed unhappiness with his current relationship and I said I was still in love with him, he didn't instantly shut me down. We were walking around at Disneyland, one of Robert's favorite places on earth. "You know, Paul," he said, "of all the times you've asked me to come back to you, this is the first time I believe it could possibly work."

He wanted to visit some friends in Las Vegas, so before he flew back to Hawaii, he drove to Sin City with me for a week. Rather than stay with me at Carla's, he stayed at his former roommate Mike's apartment. Loathe to spend even a minute apart from Robert, I invited myself to stay over at Mike's every night with him. I told him how glad I was we'd reconnected, but also that we'd had the time apart to grow into our own selves. "Massage school only lasts until May," I mentioned as we were lying in bed together one night. "I could move to Hawaii when I'm done. Start work as a therapist there."

"Maybe," he said. "Let's not make such big plans yet. There's time."

"Yes," I agreed. "We can see where we are then." I was just happy he was even entertaining the notion.

A little while later, Robert sat up in bed.

"Everything okay?" I asked.

"I'm just having one of my heart things." He meant his arrhythmia, which he'd had since he was born. Sitting up helped his heart to slow down. It did, and we went to sleep.

The next morning, Robert said since we'd spent nearly every day and night together, he wanted some time just with Mike, his old roommate. They planned to get a room on the Strip and party with ecstasy. "Fine by me," I lied, since I desperately wanted to go out with them. Out of respect for his request, though, I lamely said, "It's Sunday, anyway; I have school tomorrow morning. But if you and Mike want massages later, just call me. I'll bring my table over." We hugged goodbye.

When I didn't hear from him, around 10:00 p.m. that night I turned my phone off. I awoke after a full night's beauty rest to two voicemails from Mike. *Odd*, I thought, pressing play on his messages. *If they wanted me to come over, why did Mike call and not Robert?*

The first message started playing. "Paul, it's Mike." He was crying. "Robert stopped breathing. There's an ambulance on the way."

Oh, my God. What happened? Where are they now?

Second message. "Paul, it's Mike again. Call me as soon as you get this."

With trembling fingers, I redialed his number. He picked up, but the call dropped. I tried again. Mike answered crying. "Robert died," he said.

"Excuse me?" If this was some kind of sick joke …

"Robert died last night. We were partying and he stopped breathing and turned blue. The paramedics couldn't revive him. I'm sorry. I need you to call his moms."

"No. No way, I can't do that. You'll have to call them." I gave him Robert's moms' number and hung up.

In shock, I called my friend Amber, who'd since moved to Nevada and now lived twenty minutes away in Boulder City. "I'm coming over," she said. "Don't go anywhere. Don't do anything stupid, Paul."

As soon as I got off the phone with her, Robert's mom Nancy called. She was hysterical. "We're getting in the car now, Paul," she said, "but it takes four hours to get there. I hate to have to ask you this, but would you go to the morgue to identify Robert's body? It would speed up the process, so we can get him back sooner."

"Yes," I agreed, still in shock. I'd go with Amber whenever she got there. I went to take a shower, and something about the hot, pounding water snapped me out of it. The skin is the body's biggest organ, and mine is extra sensitive to begin with; my senses were quickly overwhelmed. Anger welled up from the deepest depths of me. I fell to the bottom of the tub yelling NO. How could our chance to be together have been snatched away so quickly, just like that?

I was still a mess when Amber arrived. As she drove us to the morgue in her jeep, I said I didn't know if I could identify him. My phone rang again: another mutual friend, who'd just received the news. "What if it's all a mistake?" she asked. "Could somebody have gotten it wrong?" I clung to this thought the rest of the way there, hoping against hope.

The coroner said if I wanted, I could identify Robert by his driver's license. A small blessing, as it meant I would get to remember him as he'd looked the last time we'd hugged goodbye. Only, when they handed me the license and I saw his face looking back at me, I lost it again. My heart broke. My world collapsed. I went back home and waited for his moms; I didn't go to school that day.

Cold

Robert Franklin died on December 8, 2008. He was twenty-nine years old.

That Thursday, my cousin Lynn, Aunt Jessica's daughter, called to let me know they'd rushed Aunt Jessica to the hospital. Technically in her fourth year of remission from pancreatic cancer, that spring they'd found spots on her lungs. She'd had surgery to remove them, but something else must have gone undetected, because according to Lynn, she was in bad shape. "If you want to see her alive," she said, "leave now."

I raced to the airport and caught the next flight to McAllen. At the hospital, I located her room and a heavily sedated Aunt Jessica. I stayed the night with her in the ICU. Once it was just the two of us, I told her how much I loved her, and how much she'd always meant to me. Holding her hand, I realized how cold it was in the room. Something told me to look in the bag next to her bed, where I found a pair of socks from Gap. "Put them on," she seemed to be saying, "so you won't be cold." I did, and I knew she was there with me.[77]

---

[77] I kept the socks. Any time I'm going through a stressful event, I wear them to remind myself I'm not alone.

The next morning, the family gathered at the hospital: Gramaw and Grampa Green, Aunt Jessica's husband, her kids. They made the difficult decision to take her off of life support, so she wouldn't have to suffer any longer. All of us stayed with her until she passed. It seemed to happen in slow motion, and was horrible and beautiful at the same time. I was devastated to lose her (and so soon after Robert), but so, so happy I'd gotten to be there with her. I stayed in Texas for her funeral, then flew back to Vegas, picked up my Ford Expedition, and drove to California for Robert's memorial.

That drive was likely the worst of my life. Sadness engulfed me. It hung from me—from my shoulders, my hips, my earlobes, my very lungs—like leaded weights. It was hard to move. Harder to breathe.

If Aunt Jessica's funeral had been painful, Robert's memorial seemed surreal. I couldn't believe I was there—that he was gone—that my heart could keep breaking into smaller and smaller pieces. It didn't feel like there was anything left to break. I stood up to speak and lost it. Eulogizing my best friend and lover tops the list of Most Difficult Things I've Ever Done. Christmas (which both Aunt Jessica and Robert had loved) wasn't worth celebrating that year. The two brightest stars of my life had blazed out. I would dread the holidays for years to come.

Beginning in 2009, when the whole world was depressed in the midst of the economic recession, and I was depressed for several reasons besides, I would become suicidal. The shock of these deaths would finally sink in, and I'd be left adrift. Or to extend our car metaphor a little further here—*drifting*.

Drifting is when a driver oversteers around a corner. She or he loses traction. The back of the vehicle slides. That was me: carried along by my own momentum, and unable in the moment to regain control. Tellingly, I couldn't have cared less.

16

Letting Go

March 2009. I was sad. Struggling to focus on massage school. Taking too many pain meds (for my back, but also because of *The Pain*). Crying to Celine Dion's "All by Myself." Feeling sensitive and temperamental. I took out the handgun I kept locked in a case in my car and stared at it, while I imagined putting it in my mouth and pulling the trigger.

I didn't pull the trigger—but the thought scared me so much I called Amber and asked her to keep the gun for me, until I felt strong enough to trust myself again. When I told my therapist what I'd done, she started me on antidepressants. At which point, I didn't feel sad anymore. But I didn't feel happy, either, only numb.

Stability would have served me best here, but stability was in short supply. Carla, I learned, was pregnant again. She needed my room for the nanny; I'd have to find somewhere else to live. Luckily, one of my private yoga clients offered me the spare bedroom in her house, just until I could graduate and start working. Then Jeffrey contacted me out of the blue. He was coming to Las Vegas. Would I like to join him and some of his friends for dinner at Encore? The very thought of seeing him again, plus his brother, his brother's wife, and even his old hairdresser Ruth and her husband, gave me a pit in the middle of my stomach. But the combined excitement and nervousness was more emotion, period, than I'd felt since starting antidepressants. Surely that was a good thing?

Dinner went well. It was nice to see everyone. Ruth commented how refreshing it was that I didn't have to excuse myself to the bathroom several times for a line or a pill, like I used to. After dinner, the two couples left to gamble and Jeffrey and I went back to his room. I set up my massage table to give him a massage. One thing led to another. I spent the night. The next morning, instead of feeling vindicated or even validated, I felt like just another trick. I vowed not to sleep with Jeffrey again, and indeed, it would be the last time I saw him for a while.

Mom came out for my graduation in May. She wanted to see Carla, whom she'd previously met in Salt Lake, and she also wanted to support me. Her support, however, emerged as concern, and I let her doubts for me weasel their way inside my head. "What are you going to do now, Paul?" she wanted to know. "Massage doesn't pay the kind of money you're used to."

"You know what?" I challenged, trying to stay brave when in reality I shared her fears. "I've always done what feels right to me, and doors have opened for me because of that. I'm following my heart. I'll get where I need to go."

And, reader, I did. Mostly because I enjoyed doing massage so much. Unlike being a car salesman, wherein you sell someone a car and rarely see them again, being a massage therapist allowed me to develop ongoing and meaningful relationships with my clients. I treated people on my table who were healing after car accidents or other injuries. For many of them, I became like a talk therapist, too. For others, massage was about receiving touch. So many of us go about our days never touching or being touched by another living person. It's important, and in helping them, I also helped myself.

Sometime in Summer 2009, I went home to visit family. I flew to Austin, met up with Mom in San Marcos, then drove with her to Gramaw and Grampa's in McAllen. The five-hour drive gave us time to catch up. She filled me in on her new boyfriend, and when she was done, I started telling her about the new guy I was interested in. My mistake. She blew up about how I was trying to "ram my gay lifestyle down her throat." I gave her high blood pressure, she said. I made her life miserable. Even though *she'd* just told me all about *her* dating life, I dropped it. Clearly, I'd been wrong to think the years had softened her stance.

When I got back to Vegas, I thought long and hard about our confrontation. It made me angry. *Let me get this straight. You can live in a house paid for by "gay" money, but you don't want to hear about it?* I upset myself so badly going round and round with my feelings that I decided to stop paying her back the thousands I still owed toward my bankruptcy attorney's fees and yoga school in Costa Rica. It was "gay" money, after all.

Quietly, I missed the next month's payment. Mom sent me a friendly reminder email. I stewed. One of the side effects of Vicodin is irrational outbursts of anger. The smallest things— and this was a big one—set me off. Finally, I sat down and poured everything I was feeling into an email. I outlined all the ways she'd wronged me in my life; how she cared about money more than her son. "I'm accepting of myself, but you can't accept me," I observed. What all that blame and vitriol amounted to was: *I won't be paying you back. Take what I owe you out of my inheritance, to include the house I paid for originally.* I clicked the send button from a place of hurt and rejection, and while I regret it today, I couldn't stop myself at the time. My mother and I quit talking for three years.

Right after this, I was forced to sell the Austin duplex. I lost one of my renters, and unable to quickly replace them from afar, I listed the property. My REALTOR suggested a fire sale price, and it went under contract almost immediately. I hated losing that duplex, but I'd been treading water with it for so long I had to let go and move on.

Accumulated Crap

By 2010, my massage therapy practice was in full swing. I'd moved into a rental house in Vegas with a friend from massage school, and incorporated a new nutritional supplement (Amber sold me on it) that had jumpstarted my efforts to get back in shape. I weaned myself off the antidepressants and the Vicodin, and as early as September 2010, believed I had made a total comeback. Life was good again. I took back my gun.

Around this time, I read the self-help book *The Secret*. I learned about the Law of Attraction, and how the things we dwell on can become self-fulfilling prophecies. When you think positive thoughts, you attract positive experiences, and vice versa. I already knew a similar principle from yoga— *Thoughts create reality*. After being reminded of this, I made a conscious effort to realign my thoughts, choosing to look at "saying goodbye" to something or someone not as "losing" them, but as "making room" for other things and people. The first way I implemented *The Secret* was by cleaning out my garage.

Able to think and see clearly for the first time in years, I suddenly noticed the boxes of accumulated crap I'd been lugging around with me from place to place—the ephemera of my former life. Most of it was jewelry and other gifts from Jeffrey or his friends, items I rarely wore or displayed but which were still worth a lot of money. Over the course of a liberating eighteen months, I sold most of these things on eBay. I researched comparable items to price them properly, then packed them with care and shipped them off with love to owners who would treasure them more than I could. Not only did the process cleanse my karma, the money I made helped me save for the next step, which I'd already decided was moving back to California.

The one memento I held onto was the green diamond. You'll recall I gave it to Jeffrey as collateral against the $125,000 loan he'd made me to get Leo and World Wide Internet off my back. I'd made payments to him totaling only a few thousand dollars when Jeffrey told me the loan was forgiven and he wanted me to have the ring back. I'd held onto it ever since, hoping one day we might use it again. I knew now we wouldn't, and I'd do well to sever this final link. In late 2010, I sent the ring to OC Tanner in Salt Lake City and had it appraised. Jeffrey had paid 90,000 sterling pounds in 1996, but fourteen years (and an economic downturn) later, it was worth a paltry $14,000. Upon my request and out of the kindness of his heart, Jeffrey contacted David Morris, the London jeweler who'd sold us the ring, for another opinion. *There are simply no buyers,* came the disheartening response.

So, Jeffrey offered to buy the ring from me. "I'll just hold onto it and sell it at a later date," he said. I was grateful, as the extra $14,000 would be enough to get me out of Vegas. The day before Thanksgiving 2011, though, Jeffrey emailed to let me know he'd changed his mind. After speaking with OC Tanner himself, he wrote, it seemed a bad investment. "You should try eBay," he suggested. Rather than let his decision derail me, I consigned the ring with Christie's in New York. They auctioned it off in Spring 2012. I pocketed $27,000, and reminded myself it was a process: Naturally, some things would be harder to let go of than others.

Las Vegas wasn't one of them. When I left Sin City for my old WeHo stomping grounds in August 2012, I didn't look back. I loved California as much as I had the first time, though I was determined not to succumb to the sundry temptations of its party scene. My family and friends were surprised. Why, now that everything was good for me again, would I jump right back into the frying pan?

"It's the only way I can prove to myself I really have changed," I told them. *And you have,* I counseled myself. *You're a survivor. You can do anything.*

I am a survivor. In the middle of drifting around life's corner, out of control and at risk of sliding right off the track, I suddenly regained traction. I found my determination, and with it, my footing. I flew back into the fast lane. Only this time, the goal wasn't to beat my previous party record. It was to chart a personal best on a new course, bypassing the bars and the clubs as I zoomed toward a different destiny. I reconnected with old friends, and hiked LA's beautiful canyons (the ones I barely noticed previously while driving home drunk or high as the sun crept over the horizon). I fed my soul Kelly Clarkson's "Stronger" and believed I was. Best of all, I appreciated what I had, instead of worrying about what else I might be missing out on.

From here on out, I thought, my life will be all the good and none of the bad.

Katy

Around this time, a friend encouraged me to sign up for a Landmark Education course. Landmark is a San Francisco company that offers personal development seminars, and in 2012, that's what I felt I needed to further my "new life of enlightenment." At my first class, a two-day intensive retreat, I learned how my fractured relationship with my mother was preventing me from moving forward in my life. I realized I *did* care about her and what she thought, independent of the belief system shaping her perspectives. Realizing this made me want to release the grudge I'd been harboring toward her and reach out to reconnect.

On the afternoon of the second day, I called her from the training—the first time I'd called her in three years, and she answered. I apologized for letting my anger come between us, and acknowledged that her rejection of me stemmed not from malice, but her fear of what would happen to me. Mom responded well. She accepted my apology and said she, too, would like to put the past behind us. I cried on the phone with her (significant, as neither of us were openly emotional people; in any other situation, we both would have perceived tears as a sign of weakness). It was one of the best things to happen to me in LA. Regardless of whether she ever accepts me 100%, today I'm happy with whatever she can give.[78]

All the while, I continued practicing yoga and massage, teaching classes and offering bodywork to the LA community. After being outside the auto industry for several years, though, I wanted to give it another shot. So I quit those pursuits and took a job with Audi Beverly Hills that proved a challenging but satisfying counterpoint to my more holistic work. The only downside was it meant being on my feet again all day every day. Soon, my back pain recurred. Against my better judgment, I ordered a refill on my Vicodin prescription through the VA, and took just half a pill as-needed. *It's okay*, I told myself. *You're not partying anymore. You love your job. This helps you show up.*

I truly enjoyed getting back into the car business. It turned out my passion for luxury cars was alive and well. After a few months, though, I decided to move back to Austin. Now that Mom and I were in each other's lives again, I wanted to reconnect with Pete and Joy as well—especially their kids. I figured I was too old to have kids myself, and they seemed financially unfeasible, anyway. My niece Katy was thriving, thwarting everyone's expectations. She'd become a big sister to my nephew Logan. Pete and his wife had had a daughter named Gracie. I was spending a lot of time and money traveling to Texas for holidays, birthdays, and other family functions. In the end, it made more sense to live in Texas than keep missing out on their lives. Besides, I'd done what I'd come to California

---

[78] I wrote Jeffrey a letter at Landmark, too—but I didn't send it. The process itself was cathartic enough to finally lay that ghost to rest.

to do: prove to myself I could live in the garden of Eden and not eat the shiny red apple. I was glad I did it. I'd never have to second-guess that decision. I was equally glad I gave it up, though, because just two short years after I returned to the Live Music Capital of the World, Katy died.

We still didn't know, when she passed, how much she could see or hear, or what, if anything, Katy made of the world and the people around her. Her existence was confined to a hospital bed, and a G-tube kept her fed. But I hope she knew how much she was loved. And that she'd singlehandedly helped my mother become the best version of herself. Jean Flamer was the patient, nurturing (grand)mother to Katy that Pete, me, and Joy had deserved.[79] Katy brought that out in her, and for that I'll always be thankful.

Say Your Piece

Jesse Leroy Green, my mom's dad, died in 2012. His wife, Mary Mildred Williams Green, passed three years after that. They went to their graves asking their out gay grandson when he was going to meet a nice girl. At least they were consistent.

Grampa was already sick in March 2012. He'd had two quadruple bypass surgeries and needed another, but at ninety he was just too weak. They didn't know how long he was going to last. I was about to leave the country for a month, en route to Mardi Gras in Australia, and decided I'd better make the five-hour trip to McAllen first—just in case.

Knowing it could be the last time we saw each other, Grampa and I began our awkward goodbyes. We still had some

---

[79] Mom even wrote and published a children's book in 2020 called *If Katy Could Talk* in her granddaughter's memory. For more information, see: https://ifkatycouldtalk.com/

unfinished business, as evidenced by Grampa's pronouncement from his hospital bed, "I just don't understand the physical things two gay men do. I can't wrap my head around how it works."

I remember telling him, "First off, you don't have to understand it, Grampa. But also, there are things you and Gramaw do that I don't want to know about, either!"

We laughed and changed the topic—probably to something about cars. While he and Gramaw never accepted me fully, it was, I believe, because they didn't know how to. Gayness didn't fit into their worldview. What they did know how to do, though, was love me, and hope only and always for my happiness.

Five days before I was scheduled to fly home from Australia, Grampa Green breathed his last. I thought about changing my ticket to make the funeral, but it would have cost a couple thousand dollars. *You know, he's not there anymore*, I reasoned to myself. *You got to say your piece before you left.* I decided to keep my original ticket, and go straight to Gramaw's when I got home. *She's the one who will need comforting now.*

Two years later, when it became apparent that Gramaw was fading fast, I once again dropped everything to be by her side. Her daughter (my mother) declined to visit. "Let me know when the funeral is," she said, "and I'll be there"—but she didn't want to see her mother while she was still alive. She respected Gramaw Green, but there was no love lost there. So, Gramaw died in the arms of her grandson, the one she'd kept hoping would magically not be gay someday. It's a funny truism of life that in your final months, weeks, or days, the bullshit that drove your whole life doesn't matter anymore. It didn't matter to Gramaw that I was gay, and it didn't matter to me that Gramaw wanted me to be something I'm not. I adored her, and I'm glad I could be there. If my mom ever gets sick and we know it's terminal, I'll show up for her, too.

In 2020, my uncle Jesse (Grampa and Gramaw Green's son—my mother's brother) passed away. Like most of the men in our family, he served in the military. I inherited the flag they draped over his coffin at the funeral (which was actually the same flag placed on Grampa Green's casket) to remember him by. Jesse had been living in Grampa and Gramaw Green's house in McAllen since their deaths. His wife, my aunt Margaret, still lives there today. Should she decide to sell the house, a small but significant piece of my childhood will go with it.

It's never easy to say goodbye—to people, to the places that remind us of them, or to the sentimental objects (like my wedding ring) we associate with them. At the same time, a clean break can be a way to let the past rest in peace, while welcoming what comes next. If possible, wait to make the break until you're less emotional, so you don't regret certain actions (again, like selling my wedding ring). Treat life instead like an endurance race, wherein teams of multiple drivers attempt to cover a large distance in a single event. You may have parted with someone or something, but as far as any of us can know, we're all still in it for the long haul. Each time we start over is an opportunity for new professions, new friends, and continued growth.

17

Perfectly Flawed

When I moved back to Austin, I initially tried transferring from the Audi dealership in LA to the one here. Audi of North Austin had promised me an interview, but they were going through a management change at the time and the woman in charge proved hard to contact. I kept after her, though, and finally they called me in. It was a man who ultimately interviewed me. We went through the standard rigmarole, but it turned out to be a waste of time. The background check the company ran on me revealed a misdemeanor from September 2012—the first month of my most recent stint in LA.

Long story short, that month I'd driven from LA to Las Vegas to visit friends and work on massage clients, and one night several of us went out drinking. I drank too many vodka-Red Bulls, tried to drive myself home, and ended up pulling over twice to puke my guts out. The second time I pulled over, a cop pulled up behind me and arrested me for DUI (later reduced to obstruction of highway). Because I'd just recently moved to California, still had an active Nevada driver's license, and was at that moment in Nevada, the charge went on my Nevada criminal history. I never imagined it would appear on a background check for a job two states later.

As a result, I didn't get the job at Audi. Instead I took a job at Toyota, where you have to work twelve-hour shifts and sell twenty-one cars a month to make a paycheck. Four months later, I'd had as much as I could take, and started applying to all the other dealerships in town. Land Rover and Mercedes both offered me interviews. I did both, and they both offered me jobs. Mercedes made me a better offer, with a guaranteed monthly minimum salary, so I took it and quit Toyota. I've never felt such smug satisfaction at quitting a job.

As it turned out, my general manager at Mercedes knew my manager at Audi Beverly Hills, which is why she'd felt so confident making me such a good offer. We entered a fruitful partnership for the next three years. Between 2013 and 2016, I earned six figures a year talking and selling luxury cars. *Swoon!* There was just one problem. Sometimes, the tendencies that emerge and the habits that get engrained in childhood never really leave us. On the Mercedes-Benz of Austin lot, Young Paul, who'd been driven to succeed at any cost, who'd wanted so badly to be perfect for his mother, who'd worked eighty hours a week for Domino's Pizza, and who'd aged a decade keeping Platinum Motors afloat for half that time, reared up. Suddenly, earning six figures wasn't enough. I wanted to be the number one salesman at the dealership. In the state. In the country.

I pushed myself, coming in early and staying late. Monday through Saturday I walked the lot, only taking Sundays off to recuperate. It wasn't only that I wanted the recognition. I was also driven by fear. Here I was, forty-something and just now opening my first 401(k). At some point, I'd need to retire, but I'd done nothing so far to get ready for that day.

Feeling behind the eight ball, and like I had no choice but to work my ass off, I stopped taking care of myself again. Walking the lot all day every day caused my back pain to flare up, underscoring my dependency on pain pills. Vicodin isn't meant to be taken long-term, but ten years after hitting my head, I was still using it. My physical body, and especially my nervous system, began to deteriorate rapidly, such that in my first year at Mercedes-Benz I probably lost ten pounds.

The person who pointed out my pants were falling off of me was himself an ex-heroin addict and opioid user. *If this guy has noticed it*, I thought, *I guess it's serious.* But I already knew that. Deep down, in a place I wouldn't admit to myself, I'd stuffed my concerns about the mini "seizures" I would occasionally experience on my way into work. I'd be driving and suddenly my eyes would feel like they were vibrating. My heart rate would increase and I'd wonder if I could complete the five-mile commute safely.

One morning in June 2016, I had a complete out-of-body experience. As was my habit, upon waking up I'd taken a 900 mg ibuprofen—my first defense against the pain. When that didn't work, I took a Vicodin. Normally, I would have juiced in the middle or downed a quick bowl of cereal, but this morning for whatever reason I skipped breakfast.

Well, something about combining the two drugs without any food made me sicker than I've ever been. The room started spinning around me. Dizzy, I sat down. Even while stable in a stationary chair, though, it seemed like at any moment I'd lose my equilibrium and fall over. Next, I had what I can only describe as an out-of-body experience. I literally felt as though my conscious self was leaving its flesh-and-blood cage behind. My skin was peeling back and I was emerging, a butterfly (but crippled) from the cocoon.

Was I going crazy?

Under other circumstances, I would have taken a Klonopin here. My trusty anxiety meds never failed me. But every good hypochondriac knows you can't mix Vicodin, an opioid depressant, with a benzodiazepine depressant (i.e., Klonopin)—not unless you want to kill yourself.

A shower, I decided, *that's what I need.*

Except, when the water hit my skin, it was immediate sensory overload. Just like it had after receiving word of Robert's death, the shower made me freak out even more. My breathing grew more labored and erratic. My heart felt like it was going to explode. I finished showering as quickly as I could, got out, and dried off, reminding myself: *You have to go to work. Pull yourself together. You have to go to work. Calm down, Paul.*

It was the last time I ever took Vicodin.

You're supposed to stop using an opioid gradually. But fuck that; I quit cold turkey. The mere memory of how it felt to be clawing my way out of my own body was reason enough not to go back.

But quitting so suddenly launches you full-tilt into withdrawal. Your body craves the drug, and when it can't get it, you start sweating. The heart palpitations begin and don't stop. You're dizzy all of the time. It's like having a days-long panic attack. You question whether it was happening beneath the surface all along, and only your daily Vicodin dose was smothering it (but never actually killing it off).

I managed by taking a Klonopin daily instead, and by not telling anyone around me what was really going on. I went to work, I focused on work, and when a week went by and I was still alive, I tried to relax. Over the next couple of months, though, I'd occasionally wake up without warning and feel like my heart was pounding right out of my chest. Or my stomach would hurt so badly I believed I was dying. Twice within the first two months I drove myself to the emergency room. Both times they failed to find anything "wrong" with me. "It appears to be stress," they said. "Just take a Klonopin."

For the first time in my life, I could commiserate with the homeless people I saw muttering to themselves on Austin's street corners and under its bridges. That's what I feared was happening to me. I was shaking my head and talking to myself, scared to death I'd lose my job, cause a car wreck, or worse, forget who I was. The constant dizziness alone was enough to make me feel like I'd lost all control. Would I ever get better? Was this my new normal?

That was four years ago. Things are much better now. Some mornings I still wake up wondering *Am I going to be okay today?*

But I try to limit my Klonopin usage to those times I really need it. The drug makes me tired, so on those days my options are basically being anxious or being exhausted. At the time of writing this, I haven't taken a single Klonopin in three months. Just knowing I can take one if I need to calms my anxious brain. I also see an acupuncturist and a naturopath these days, both of whom are helping me, too. I'm not 100% yet, but someday I hope to be.

A Game Changer

I left Mercedes-Benz in September 2017, after they rewarded my outstanding salesmanship with a pay cut. One of my really good friends (Shawn) who'd been with Mercedes for about a year said, "This is ridiculous. There's no money in the car business anymore. Let's sell houses."[80] So, we looked around, applied to a couple places, and eventually both got hired at the same company.

Shawn got the job with the new home builder first, and referred me a month later. Originally, I was scared to take it. Sure, both cars and homes are sales positions with similar work-day structures, but the products are completely different, as are the sales processes. To learn them, I'd have to attend a multi-day training in Houston—entirely out of my comfort zone. "I don't know if I can do this," I told Shawn.

"You're going to be okay," he assured me. "Just hang in there. Have you spoken to Serena lately?"

---

[80] Not only was the auto industry tanking as it shifted to a volume model, but my acupuncturist recommended I get out, too. "That environment is toxic for you," she told me more than once. "I know you're making good money, but it's not healthy. You're killing yourself!" Thank you, Denise, for caring. Anymore, I make sure I take my two days off every week!

Serena is one of the many holistic practitioners I employ to help me navigate life these days. I consider her a friend and spiritual guide, and I lean on her any time I have to make a big decision. She never tells me what to do—she merely helps me assess the options I present and select which one stands the highest chance of success or will most contribute to my overall happiness. Serena is the one who told me to take the job with the new home builder. "It's a good move," she said. "You should do it."

So, at Shawn's prompting, I talked to Serena before the training in Houston. She pepped me up and got me excited about the opportunity to meet new people and learn new things. Later, when the new home builder assigned me the furthest possible community from my South Austin residence, ratcheting up my road anxiety (one of the less desirable side effects of quitting Vicodin cold turkey was my developing claustrophobia in cars[81]), Serena recommended liquid lecithin. "You can get a bottle at GNC for ten dollars," she said. "Take one teaspoon every morning for your anxiety." Having nothing to lose, I tried it and it worked! Lecithin calms the nervous system—and by extension, calmed *me*—by coating the ends of each nerve, so they're not constantly inflamed and firing. It was a real game changer for me.

By Summer 2019, I finally felt able to drive comfortably again. The new home builder had assigned me a new community, shortening my hour commute by half, and now I could arrive at my destination *not* soaked in sweat or scrambling to get out

---

[81] When I say "claustrophobia," I mean I started blasting my air conditioning on high in the middle of winter because I would get so hot. I had to turn the radio, normally a source of comfort for me, off completely—no distractions. I drove in the right hand lane exclusively in case I needed to pull over and breathe. All because Austin has some of the worst traffic in the country, and without the drug my body had been dependent on for so long, it basically ceased functioning there for a while.

of the car. I didn't have to show up at my office and try to hide from my coworkers how scattered and dizzy I felt. Serena's assistance was invaluable to me.

Around this time, I also started seeing a naturopathic doctor. This particular doctor came recommended by a friend from my men's yoga class, who sagely said, "There's always someone ready to help you; you just have to be receptive to it." Doctor Chad put me on several herbs, enzymes, and superfood supplements (spirulina, beets) based on a hair test that revealed calcium and magnesium deficiencies, among other low vitamin/mineral levels. Most fascinating, he read my birth chart. I was reminded that I'm passionate, romantic, sensitive, loyal to those I love, and empathic—meaning, I pick up on others' feelings and can often physically experience what they're feeling in my own body. I find emotional fulfillment in helping others, and I'm extremely strong and resilient. "You can literally take a beating and bounce back from almost anything," he said.

While these qualities resonate with me and I recognize them as true, all "good" qualities have their downsides, too. If I'm not careful to keep myself grounded, for example, via yoga and massage and other self-care routines, I can easily be overwhelmed by my empathic response to those around me. And although I love helping others, if I'm not discerning, it can lead to me being taken advantage of (which I'd say we've seen throughout this book, no?). Knowing these things about myself allows me to make informed decisions, protect myself, and also give of myself, should I so choose, in meaningful ways. All of which in turn contributes to my innate "strength and resilience."

I still talk to Serena once a month and see my naturopath every two weeks. I see a chiropractor once every six weeks, and an acupuncturist every two weeks as well. Between all these guides and my own practice of meditation and yoga, I'm able to function again, and participate in things outside my comfort zone. In October 2019, I went on a cruise to Mexico where I knew two out of the three thousand people on board.[82] Maybe that sounds like no big deal for someone who once loved getting lost in the crowds at Mardi Gras, but I really did go through something akin to a mid-life crisis (or one prolonged panic attack) in the years after quitting Vicodin. It's been difficult, but I've come a long way.

I call the group of people here in Austin who work to keep me happy, healthy, and sane my "team." Included among their ranks are Pete and Joy, the only two people who have been there for me from the beginning.

These days, we try to get together monthly. Joy drives up from San Antonio, where she lives now with her son Logan, and Pete will join us with or without his new wife Rachel. Sometimes we invite the cousins who live in the area, too. Over Christmas last year (2019), we threw a joint birthday party for my mom and Pete's daughter Gracie. Mom hosted and cooked dinner for everyone. Afterward, she sent me a note thanking me for the presents. "You're a very special person and I'm so glad that you're my son," it read. That was really sweet. While it's not perfect, we continue working on our relationship every day. I also try and keep in touch with my dad's side of the family, visiting my uncle Irv (my dad's brother) and my aunt Sharon (Irv's wife) as often as I can. We recently took a cruise for a family vacation to celebrate my cousin Neil's fiftieth birthday. Even with all our busy schedules, we do our best to stay in touch as much as possible.

At the same time, I have this thing called a job that's very time-consuming, and my brother and sister are busy with their lives as well. So we don't get together as often as I imagined we would when I first moved back to Austin. It's okay, though,

---

[82] I also read Elton John's new memoir *Me* on board, and highly recommend it. The similarities between our stories, including our parallel drug use, is what caused me to want to finish my book.

because sometimes I just want to go home and do nothing. Not talk to anyone, or feel like I have to be "on." Time for me to recharge. I used to stay up all night partying to forget who I was. I guess the billionaire's brat is catching up on lost sleep now, so he can become who he knows he can be.

Personal Pride Fest

I truly feel I'm where I need to be, doing the things I want to do, here in Austin today. I feel more supported than ever, and consequently, able to give more support to those I love in return. It seems to me that life is like school. We progress through the grades, studying and mastering whatever we came here to learn—which for most of us, I think, is learning to love our flawed yet perfect selves. Some of us need two years of school; some of us need eighty years. Once we are done with "school," we go on to the next phase, which may or may not be in this physical realm. Call it heaven if you wish, I don't care. The only things I'm certain of are that it's not the end, and it's not a wholly separate place. How do I know? Because my whole life, there have been angels all around me.

Currently, I don't go to church. I believe there's a God. I believe He created us. I believe He loves me always. Whether I go to church does not predetermine my ability to be a good person. For so long, church was the enemy. They threw me out. They told me I was an abomination. But if I look at it like school, and question what lesson that experience had to teach me, then I see how it forced me to seek out the people who would accept me, who would help me become that good person, the one who doesn't live in resentment but gratitude for the fires that forged me.

Same with Leo, and the Hoggs—those who took advantage of me, and profited from my naïveté. By nature I'm trusting and want to be optimistic. I want things to work out, so I go for it, even when it seems I should have learned from past mistakes. Because I can go around wondering *When's that piano going to fall out of the sky and crush me?* or I can crush life. Trusting the world to cushion my fall, to catch that wayward piano, has taught me I always bounce back. You end up on your feet when you keep putting one in front of the other.

My anxiety complicates the progress. It's noisy all the time in my head. There were years when drugs muffled the noise, when "hot mess" would have been a generous descriptor. Then yoga and breath work helped me to separate from the craziness of the outside world and focus on the reality at hand. I'm still a pleaser, but now I know to put my own oxygen mask on first before trying to help other people. In the past, I helped others so much I hurt myself. My tank was empty, and still I was towing them out of the mud.

To an extent, I regret the pain I caused myself, like I regret the pain I caused those I care about. There are things I said to Jeffrey I wish I could take back. I never should have sent that damning letter to my mother. But I did. I wasn't mature enough. And anyway, you can't put the genie back in the bottle.

So, I focus on repairing what I can. Or making good by showing compassion to strangers. You never know what someone's going through, especially if they're a member of the LGBT community. Let's give high-fives to those living loud and proud, and be the chosen families for those who don't have them. Support Out Youth, an organization sheltering kids of all sexual orientations and gender identities in Austin. Live every day like it's your personal Pride fest.

Then settle into your touring vehicle for the cross-country drive—something big, fast, comfortable, and easy to see you through the long haul. You'll still have to stop for gas, do routine maintenance, and change your oil like Grampa taught you. But most of the time, it's okay to relax and cruise along, singing the refrain to George Michael's "Flawless" and taking in the view outside the window.

Afterword

It was almost ten years ago, in 2010, that I first got the idea to write this book. I was forty years old then, and although I felt fulfilled working as a massage therapist in Las Vegas, two other factors conspired to make me think it was time. First, my flexible massage schedule meant I had some extra hours here and there. Second—and more crucially—I believed I'd gained enough distance from my story to commit it pretty objectively to paper. So, I started researching, intent on reconstructing vivid descriptions and an accurate timeline of events. I went back to Utah. I visited Jeffrey. I drove around base. I reached out to everyone from my past I was still in contact with and asked them to share with me what they remembered. It helped that I'm a borderline hoarder and had kept every letter and photo. And finally, inspired by Steven Soderbergh's adaptation of *Behind the Candelabra: My Life with Liberace*, based on Scott Thorson's memoir of the same name,[83] I wrote.

As I soon realized, though, writing a book is a Herculean task. And I wasn't at all done processing the traumas of my past, not by a long shot. Early drafts reflected a definite victim mentality. In them, I blamed more than I sought to understand. I wrote to purge, rather than to share. And I didn't care at all how anyone else came off, or who I might be hurting with my words.

---

[83] This movie came out in 2013. I watched it on HBO and cried, feeling like so much of Thorson's story was my story, too. Along with Elton John's *Me*, *Behind the Candelabra* was a major catalyst for moving me to finish my book.

Several drafts and a decade later, I've made peace with myself, my story, and those featured in it. Both Jeffrey and my mom, the two people who stand to lose the most face here, know about this book, and Mom at least understands why I had to write it. There are things they both wish I wouldn't have written, and things all of us wish hadn't happened. But if I left those things out, it wouldn't be my story, and anyway, I'm tired of half-truths, cover-ups, and outright lies. For twenty-four years of my life, I lived a lie. No more. Meet the real Paul Flamer.

Serena, one of my holistic practitioners, encouraged me to write this book. "You'd be surprised," she said, when I asked for her opinion, "how as people get older, they soften in their stances. The things that used to bother them just don't bother them anymore." I thought of Grampa and Gramaw Green—how in their older age, they were less inclined to write me off for being gay. It's an idea that gives me hope. Maybe ten, fifteen, or twenty years from now, the belief systems my mother holds to be self-evident, the belief systems I hold to be self-evident, and even the belief systems that you, reader, hold to be self-evident, may become entirely obsolete. Because they just don't matter anymore.

On August 17, 2020, I will turn fifty years old. It's a significant milestone for me for several reasons. As the story that opened *Up in Flames* probably indicated, I never expected to live past my thirtieth birthday. At the time, I couldn't see a reason to. Now, I'm shocked to be turning fifty. On the one hand, it's a grateful kind of shocked. I'm alive, obviously, and also I've been told I don't *look* fifty years old—especially remarkable, given the substances and stress I subjected my body to over the years. But the continued fact of my existence simultaneously makes me anxious. I feel like I wasted so many years partying or goofing off. There's so much more I could have been doing to put myself in a better position for retirement, say, so I can be more financially comfortable for the long haul. I didn't take those measures because I didn't think they were necessary.

My naturopath tells me, "You can't live in the past, Paul, just like you can't live in the future. You have to live in the now." Thinking about all the things I could have done—that's living in the past. It's not helpful to me. Nor is living in the future; e.g., looking at the beautiful new house I just bought and already daydreaming about the next one. "You don't stop and revel in the things you've done," Denise, my acupuncturist reminds me. "You've done so much; you should be proud." *I know I've done so much*, I think. *But I can do more.* These are the struggles of present-day Paul, who works so he doesn't have to deal with his feelings—like the fact I haven't seriously dated anyone since Robert died, because twelve years later, my heart is still crushed.

There again is the part of me that's shocked to be turning fifty, and having to face the hard truth that I'm not getting younger, and the relationships I mourn from my past aren't coming back to save me. I'm in disbelief over a lot of it. At the same time, I relish the wisdom that comes with age. The ability to look back and recognize how the experiences of my past inform the man I am today. And the fact that if I did cash out everything I own at present, my 401(k), my other assets, I could live well for a while. Maybe not until age eighty, but that's a future concern. When I step back and look at the bigger picture, I think, *You* have *accomplished a lot, Paul.* And that's something worth celebrating.

About the Author

Paul Flamer was born and raised in Texas. He left the state to spend four years in the Air Force, the last two of which were at a base in Utah. Utah was also where he embarked upon a tumultuous relationship with a billionaire that would take him around the world several times over, with many adventures and mishaps along the way. Eventually, he ended up back in Texas, where he lives today in Austin with his lovable schnauzers Bentley and Sasha. *UP IN FLAMES* is his first book.

Resources for Support

In Texas

Equality Texas
www.equalitytexas.org
(512) 474-5475

Out Youth
www.outyouth.org
(512) 419-1233

In the United States

LGBT National Hotline
www.glbthotline.org
(888) 843-4564

The Trevor Project
www.thetrevorproject.org
(866) 488-7386

Trans Lifeline
www.translifeline.org
(877) 565-8860

Made in the USA
Monee, IL
17 August 2020